ROYAL WESTMINSTER ABBEY

Royal
Westminster Abbey

BRYAN BEVAN

LONDON
ROBERT HALE · LONDON

© Bryan Bevan 1976
First published in Great Britain 1976

ISBN 0 7091 5813 0

Robert Hale Limited
Clerkenwell House
Clerkenwell Green
London EC1R OHT

Filmset by Specialised Offset Services Limited, Liverpool
and printed in Great Britain by
Lowe & Brydone Limited
Thetford, Norfolk

Contents

Illustrations

The author wishes to thank the following for their kind permission to reproduce photographs: the National Gallery (no. 6), the President and Fellows of Queen's College, Cambridge (no. 8), Lord Brooke of Warwick Castle and the Courtauld Institute (no. 9), S. Eost and P. Macdonald (no. 11), and the Dean and Chapter of Westminster for the remaining photographs.

Acknowledgements

The author would like to express his grateful thanks to the following: the Rev. Dr Edward Carpenter, Dean of Westminster, for his advice and encouragement before the author took the plunge of writing his history; the Rev. Dr Eric Abbott, former Dean of Westminster, for his courtesy and advice. Mr Algernon Greaves, the former Dean's Verger, for his consideration, kindly interest and help at all times; Mr N.H. MacMichael, Keeper of the Muniments, Westminster Abbey Library, Mr Howard Nixon, the Librarian, and their staff for constant encouragement and courtesy at all times when he was writing the book; Dr Lawrence Tanner, former Keeper of the Muniments, Westminster Abbey Library, for his invaluable help and advice; Mr W.R.J. Pullen, Receiver General, for his sympathetic help and interest, and lastly my sister Winfreda for helping me with the page proofs.

To Cherry

Preface

While I was serving as a temporary marshal in the Abbey during
the spring and summer of 1974, I became deeply interested in its
history. No person can work there without being powerfully
influenced by its unique beauty and wonderful atmosphere. An
aspiration, vague and shadowy at first, came to me that I must
write a book, and when my duties terminated in the season of the
sere and yellow leaf I had formed a firm resolution to do so.

My theme is an important one, the theme of the monarchy in
relation to Westminster Abbey from the time of Edward the
Confessor throughout more than nine hundred years of
evolution. What immediately impressed me were the intimate
friendships forged between some of the Plantagenet kings with
the abbots of Westminster. For instance, Henry III's close
relations with Richard de Crockesley and Richard de Ware.
Many of the early abbots were great travellers, being frequently
employed on important foreign missions. Another outstanding
abbot was Nicholas Littlington, who enjoyed the friendship of
Edward III as did his predecessor Simon Langham, the only
abbot of Westminster to attain the eminent offices of Cardinal
and Archbishop of Canterbury.

John Islip enjoyed the friendship of Henry VII our first Tudor
king. When he dined at the Abbot's house, Islip's cook prepared
his marrow-bone puddings for which he was renowned. Even
today Islip's gentle, benign spirit seems to haunt the Islip Chapel,
beloved by nurses, who come there from all over the
Commonwealth.

As a marshal, one of my duties was to answer questions. These
seldom failed to stimulate me. A favourite one: "Is Henry VIII
buried here?" "No, he is buried with his third Queen in St

George's Chapel, Windsor," I would say. They were delighted when I showed them the tomb of his fourth Queen, Anne of Cleves, below the royal chair presented to Queen Elizabeth II by the Canadian government, near the High Altar. "Where are the kings and queens coronated?" our delightful visitors from overseas would enquire and I would tell them. Another question more rarely asked: "Where is King John interred?" Actually, in Worcester Cathedral. "Can you show me Sir Isaac Newton's monument or where David Livingstone is buried?" There is the never-failing variety, the desire to help and please people who may have come great distances to see one particular monument. For at least a year after she had been married in Westminster Abbey, people with a sense of wonderment flocked to see where Princess Anne had wed Mark Phillips, oblivious often of the fact that her mother and Prince Philip's wedding had also taken place there, as had her grandfather's and grandmother's in 1923.

I was once asked by a donnish-looking woman where Richard Hakluyt, who laboured tirelessly to record the voyages of the great Elizabethan seamen and navigators, was buried. He had particular associations with the Abbey, having been educated at Westminster School. He is interred in the south transept, but the exact spot is difficult to ascertain. People come from all parts of the world to see the marble stone commemorating Sir Winston Churchill, unveiled by Queen Elizabeth II (September 1965). It lies between the grave of the Unknown Warrior and the west door.

There is the memorial plaque to Franklin Delano Roosevelt near the west door. In the nave is the tablet commemorating the American George Peabody, the philanthropist, whose remains are today interred in his native state, Massachusetts. They are intrigued by the monument raised to commemorate Major John Andre, Adjutant-General of the British forces in America, captured and hanged as a British spy in 1780.

The French delight in the Abbey's architecture, reminding them of their own wonderful cathedrals of Reims or Amiens. Some of the finest works in stone are by French sculptors, such as the tomb of George Villiers, first Duke of Buckingham by Le Sueur. The Italians are keenly interested in the Cosmati work forming a pavement near the high altar brought from Rome in

the late thirteenth century by Abbot de Ware. The effigy of
Lady Margaret Beaufort in her old age by Pietro Torrigiano is
usually considered the fiery Florentine's masterpiece. German
students group together round Handel's monument.

For those seeking repose or a quiet place for prayer there is the
ancient St Faith's Chapel. Near the chapter house is the doorway
leading up to the chapter library, a place which owes much to
John Williams who became Dean in 1620.

For me Westminster Abbey has cast its spell, never ceasing to
enchant me, even if I have cursed at times its hard pavements.

1

Early Kings and Westminster Abbey

The personality of the Saxon King Edward the Confessor is of profound importance in the history of Westminster Abbey, particularly because of the love and reverence he inspired in the Plantagenet kings, Henry III, Edward I and his grandson Edward III, Richard II and Henry V.

Edward was born about A.D. 1005, the son of King Ethelred by his second marriage to his Norman wife Queen Emma. The main influence, which moulded his life, was his long exile in Normandy after his father Ethelred's death when the Danes ruled England. The name Confessor in the early Church meant one who suffered for confessing his or her faith, but only to an extent which did not involve martyrdom. Edward returned to England where he reigned for twenty-four years (1042-1066).

Most people imagine Edward as a kind of Father Christmas figure, but this impression is partly divorced from the truth. Edward was usually mild and benignant, deeply religious, and he possessed wisdom, shrewd judgement and considerable intelligence. When provoked, however, he had a hot temper. A peasant, who attempted to frustrate the King in his passion for hunting, had reason to repent it. "By God and His Mother," he fulminated, "I will give you just such another turn [punishment] if ever it come in my way." His occasional rages are reminiscent of the Plantagenet Kings Henry II and Richard II. Those who encountered Edward were sometimes surprised by his sudden merry peals of laughter. He was an enthusiast, loving to hear the baying of his hounds, but deeply conscientious in his devotional exercises. He was human enough to quarrel both with his wife Queen Edith, a daughter of the powerful Earl Godwin, and with his Norman mother Queen Emma, a dominating personality. A close study of his character makes it apparent that the King was a natural psychic. His long thin hands were those of an artist rather than a practical man of business, and his beard may have been as snowy white as tradition says, and his cheeks as flushed with red. His biographer Frank Barlow, however, wrote, "Whether Edward in 1043 was short or tall, muscular or slight, dark or fair, imposing or insignificant, is unknown."

After his father Ethelred's death, Edward had made a vow to make a pilgrimage to St Peter's grave at Rome, since Edward possessed a special veneration for St Peter. Once, however, he ascended the throne Edward was unable to leave his kingdom. The Pope then released him from his vow, provided the King promised to found or restore a monastery dedicated to St Peter.

Actually an earlier church stood a few yards to the west of the site on which the Confessor built his church. Certainly Benedictine monks had worshipped there during the later tenth century A.D., when the Saxon King Edgar was on the throne and Dunstan was Archbishop of Canterbury. There is a Westminster tradition, and it may well be true, that Sebert, King of the East Saxons, built an earlier church here. During my periods of service as a marshal in Westminster Abbey, I sometimes pointed out his grave to our visitors. The district now called Westminster was originally known as Thorney Island, for it was overgrown with thorns, and surrounded with water.

Edward was born at Islip in Oxfordshire, crowned at Winchester, and he died at Westminster. Of the earlier Saxon kings, Edgar's coronation had taken place at Bath in A.D. 973, and Edward's father Ethelred had been crowned on the coronation stone, still to be seen at Kingston-on-Thames. Edward loved Westminster, and that was the reason for his choice of this place for his church. Since he wanted to supervise the progress of the work, which was being undertaken in the monastery at Westminster, it is a reasonable surmise that Edward himself erected the palace at Westminster. That an earlier palace stood on the site is almost certain because one authority, Norden, refers to one inhabited by King Canute about 1035, which was destroyed by fire.

Edward was a ~~Saxon~~ by birth, but in building Westminster Abbey he was strongly influenced by Norman ideas. His church, which was to be rebuilt by Henry III, was designed in the Romanesque style, which had spread from Burgundy into Normandy. It was built in dressed Reigate stone, and had a long nave of six double bays, thus resembling the Norman church of Jumièges. Among its features were a lantern tower over the crossing, and a presbytery of two bays. William of Normandy always based his claims to the English throne not on rights of conquest but on Edward's alleged bequest. Norman sources maintain that Earl Godwin's son Harold was sent by Edward to William to confirm by oath the bequest of the throne, supposedly made in 1051. Yet as Edward lay dying at the beginning of January 1066, he turned to Harold and said, referring to Queen Edith now reconciled to him, "I commend this woman with all the Kingdom to your protection." Edith was as pious as her husband, and had rebuilt the nunnery at Wilton. The royal couple were childless. The minster at Westminster had only just been consecrated to the "honour of God and St Peter, and all God's Saints". Westminster Abbey is still known today as the Collegiate Church of St Peter. Edward was buried as he had desired and had intended on Thursday, 6th January 1066, before the high altar. There the Confessor lay in his royal robes, his crown upon his head, and a crucifix of gold, with a golden chain round his neck. Buried, too, in the cloisters was Hugolin, Edward's favourite chaplain and principal chamberlain, devoted servant of the King. When Westminster Abbey was rebuilt by Henry III during the thirteenth century, Hugolin's bones together with Edwin's, the first abbot of his church, were removed to a new tomb at the entrance to the chapter house.

It is probable, though by no means certain, that Harold II was crowned in Westminster Abbey on 6th January, but owing to the unusual circumstances the ceremony was very hasty, and according to an early chronicler, Matthew of Westminster, Harold placed his own crown on his head. Tradition relates that Harold was killed at the Battle of Hastings on 14th October by a Norman arrow. This is untrue, for he met his death struck down by a Norman knight.

It is related that Edward the Confessor during his lifetime was the first to touch for the King's Evil (a skin disease), and stories abounded after his death of the many miracles performed at his tomb. It now became the scene of religious manifestations.

It was extremely astute of William of Normandy – known to history as William the Conqueror – to have himself crowned at Westminster Abbey on Christmas Day 1066. The dominating, fierce William always professed a great regard for the memory of Edward the Confessor, and regarded himself, whether sincerely or not, as King of England not by victory but by right. It was absolutely necessary for him to humour his new subjects, who during the reign of the first Norman king were to look back with nostalgia to their Saxon king's reign as a kind of golden age. So he was sagacious to select this place, to be crowned beside the grave of the Confessor. Since William's time all our kings have been crowned at Westminster Abbey with the exception of Edward V, one of the Princes in the Tower, and the late Duke of Windsor, who succeeded his father as Edward VIII. Christmas Day was chosen because, like Easter and Whitsuntide it was a period of high festival when the Saxon kings had been wont to re-enact their coronations. It was a strange scene that day in Edward's Church as William I stood at the high altar together with a Norman prelate Godfrey, Bishop of Coutances, and the Saxon Aldred, Archbishop of York. It was customary for the Saxon kings to be crowned by the Archbishop of Canterbury, but Edward's Archbishop Stigand had fled to Scotland. The Norman bishop spoke French, a language understood by the Normans, while Aldred's English was for his Saxon audience. Outside the Abbey was ranged some Norman cavalry ready to enter there to quell any disturbance. One can imagine the sentiments of the Saxons, angered that they were to be ruled by William, who they regarded as an usurper. However, Aldred turned to the English nobles, saying "Are you willing to have the Duke of Normandy for your King?" The Norman cavalry outside now mistook the sounds of acclamation of those present – under duress as some of them undoubtedly were – for signs of rebellion. Brutally they entered the church, and the piercing cries of the Saxons could be heard as they were trampled on by the horses' hooves. The Normans hastily set fire to buildings in the neighbourhood of the church, which would have spread to the noble church itself had not the flames been exterminated.

Despite Duke William's toughness, his coronation must have been a fearful ordeal. Before setting the crown on his head, Aldred, who had the courage to stand up to the King on several later occasions, made William give his solemn oath that he would protect his subjects. Godfrey, Bishop of Coutances also presented the new King to his people in French.

The importance of William's coronation was that it gave sanction to the kingship he had won by arms. There was some justice in his claim that he had been formally designated by King Edward as his legitimate successor. Those who support his claim maintain that Edward's promise to Harold on his death-bed was extracted from him by duress.

The coronation of Matilda, William's Queen, took place at Winchester, the former Saxon capital of England, in 1068 at Pentecost. The liturgical acclamations, known as the *Laudes Regiae*, were first introduced by the Normans at an English coronation, though they had formed part of the service at the coronation of Charlemagne and also been sung during the chief festivals of the Church.

After his coronation William began to construct the Tower of London, so as to be able to defend the capital against rebellion and sedition. Despite his brutality, avarice and cruelty, William was in many ways a great man. His choice of the Norman Lanfranc as Archbishop of Canterbury at the age of fifty-five was a wise one, for Lanfranc was a remarkable statesman, a monk by temperament and training, a versatile lawyer, diplomatist and teacher. It was Lanfranc, with his influence over William, who persuaded him that no Archbishop of York should ever again be entrusted with the privilege of crowning kings. He argued with some vehemence that an Archbishop of York might be tempted to confer the crown on a Dane or a Scot, elected by the Saxons. The privilege must be enjoyed by Archbishops of Canterbury, and in his absence the Bishop of London must preside over the ceremony, not the Archbishop of York. The latter's main function has been the crowning of the Queen Consorts, and it was the Saxon Aldred who presided at Matilda's coronation. Towards the end of his reign, William appointed Gilbert Crispin, who came of an aristocratic Norman family, as Abbot of

Westminster. He was to prove an outstanding one. It early became the duty of Abbots of Westminster to instruct and prepare our kings for the solemnities of the coronation. Before the holy anointing – the most solemn part of the service – it was necessary for the kings to confess their sins. This ancient function of the abbots is today performed by the Deans of Westminster.

The regalia, all Anglo-Saxon, were kept in those early days in the Treasury of Westminster until the time of Henry VIII, and the larger part until the Civil War in 1642 when they were broken up. After the Restoration the new regalia were sent to the Tower where they are kept today. On the eve of a coronation they are entrusted to the care of the Deans of Westminster. The regalia consisted of the crown of Edward or Alfred for the King, and the crown of Edith, wife of the Confessor, for the Queen. The sceptre with the dove was the symbol of the peace enjoyed in his Kingdom by Edward after the expulsion of the Danes. Other coronation regalia was the ring, King Edward's ivory comb, and the orb. Today visitors to Westminster Abbey are able to see replicas of the Crown Jewels in the Abbey museum.

It was politic of King William to respect the feelings of his Saxon subjects in one important respect. When Edward's widow Edith died at Winchester just before Christmas in 1075, William ordered that her body should be borne to Westminster, where he was keeping the festival, and buried near her husband at the high altar. So, this lady, who had taken a great interest in Wilton nunnery, was given high honours at the end. Near her was laid to rest forty-three years later her namesake Edith (Matilda), Henry I's pious Saxon Queen, who died at Westminster, and who may have felt a kind of affinity with her predecessor, for she had been educated at Wilton. According to an Anglo-Saxon chronicle, Henry I was married in 1100 with great splendour to Queen Edith in Westminster Abbey.

William I died abroad in 1087, in the priory of St Gervais near Rouen. He was succeeded as King by his third and favourite son William Rufus. Historians have found hardly anything favourable to say about William II. This far from attractive man had a coarse red face, reddish hair and his curious grey eyes were deep set. He was extremely impulsive, obstinate, tyrannical and reckless. Once when his courtiers in vain tried to prevent him from crossing the Channel in a storm, William boasted "Kings never drown". His irreligion was such that he was nearly excommunicated by the Pope. Yet by a strange paradox, although not mentioned in the biographical sketch in the *Dictionary of National Biography*, it was William who during his short reign of thirteen years built Westminster Hall, one of the most beautiful architectural gems in our country. The work was begun about 1097. On one occasion when he had returned from a visit to Normandy, William Rufus inspected the Great Hall. When an attendant, possibly from a malicious motive, remarked that he thought it to be much larger than was necessary, the King curtly replied, "It is not half large enough." According to Matthew Paris writing during the reign of Henry III, almost a century and a half later, Rufus said, "It is a mere bedchamber compared with what I had intended to build." Actually William Rufus's Hall was 239 feet 6 inches long and 67 feet 6 inches wide. Both Caen stone and Reigate were used in constructing the walls. When we think of Westminster Hall, it is of the magnificent coronation banquets held there after the crowning of the Plantagenet and later kings. It was later the tragic setting, too, for dramatic trials such as that of Robert Devereux, Earl of Essex, Guy Fawkes, Charles I, and in our own time William Joyce (Lord Haw-Haw). The hammer-beam roof, which is its chief glory, was erected during the reign of Richard II towards the end of the fourteenth century. Hugh Herland, the extremely talented carpenter chiefly responsible, deserves to be far better known.

It is unlikely, however, that Rufus had any particular affection for Westminster Abbey, though he was crowned there on 26th September 1087 by Archbishop Lanfranc, assisted by the only remaining Saxon bishop, Wulfstan, bishop of Worcester.

William Rufus, as every schoolboy knows, was killed in an accident whilst hunting in the New Forest. His body was hastily taken to Winchester to be buried there. Since Rufus was a bachelor he was succeeded by his youngest brother Henry, who lost no time in making for Westminster on hearing of his brother's death. Henry I was crowned at Westminster Abbey on 5th August 1100 by Maurice, Bishop of London because Anselm, the Archbishop of Canterbury, was unable to officiate. He had quarrelled with William Rufus. Thomas, Archbishop of York, was at Ripon when he heard of Rufus's death, but he arrived too late in London to be able to claim his lost privilege to crown kings. There was no difficulty in getting Henry to swear at the altar that he would "annul all the unrighteous acts that took place in his brother's time".

Henry I was more affable than his brother William Rufus, and he lived often at the Palace of Westminster, diverting himself with his mistresses, where he sometimes held his Court. It is evident that state affairs were now transacted here, for at a great Council held at Westminster on the festival of St Michael, there were present all the chief men of England, both clergy and laity. Six years later there was a session at Westminster when he selected various candidates for bishroprics and abbacies, both in England and Normandy. The relations between Henry and the monks at Westminster Abbey were not close.

Indeed it was his Queen Edith who was more beloved. She was descended from Saxon Kings and popular with Henry's Saxon subjects, not only on account of her birth, but also because of her many virtues. According to an Anglo-Saxon chronicle, Edith was married to Henry during 1100 in Westminster Abbey, but this is doubtful. In deference to Norman prejudices she changed her name Matilda on becoming Henry's first wife. At Lent she was wont to walk barefoot from the Palace to the Abbey, in a garment of hair to hear mass and to wash the feet of the poor. She donated to the Abbey a sacred relic, a large part of the hair of Mary Magdalene. Edith had been crowned in the Abbey on 11th November 1100, just over three months after Henry I. It is possible that Henry's Queen was first buried at the entrance of the chapter house, and that Henry II later had her body removed to a position near St Edward's Shrine.

After her death, Henry married Adelicia of Louvaine, who on account of her beauty was known as "the fair Maid of Brabant". It was a great relief to his nobles, for since the death of his first wife Henry's temper had grown so violent that they hardly dared to enter his presence. Henry died suddenly in Normandy in 1135, and only one daughter by his first wife survived him. This was the Empress Matilda. Henry I was buried in Reading Abbey in which he had constantly taken a keen interest.

He was succeeded by his nephew Stephen, who was crowned

in the Abbey Church of Westminster by Archbishop William of Canterbury on St Stephen's Day, 26th December 1135. Stephen's chief importance in the history of Westminster is that he was the reputed founder of St Stephen's Chapel (the late House of Commons), dedicated in honour of the Proto-Martyr. Stephen was a grandson of William the Conqueror, a son of his daughter Adela. He was a favourite of Henry I, who after his heir William had been drowned in the White Ship, had brought him up to take his place. He married his nephew to an heiress Matilda of Boulogne, whose coronation took place in the Abbey on Easter Day, 22nd March 1136.

Stephen, the last of our Anglo-Norman kings, was neither resolute enough or tough enough to be able to stand up to the unruly barons of the early twelfth century. A mild, good man did not make a successful ruler. Stephen was buried together with his wife Matilda in Faversham Abbey.

He was succeeded by Henry II, a man of strong personality and the first of the Plantagenet kings. Henry's coronation together with his Queen Eleanor of Aquitaine on Sunday, 19th December 1154, was a splendid affair. Archbishop Theobald of Canterbury presided, assisted by his personal friend the Archbishop of York and by the Archbishop of Rouen. The antagonism between the rival sees of Canterbury and York were temporarily forgotten.

The second Henry was a remarkable ruler, a man of tremendous energy. Not only was he a gifted athlete, but he was scholarly, interested in literature, and a talented linguist. He was in the habit of sitting in judgement in person, though it was Henry who instituted legal circuits with judges of assize remote from the Court. He could hardly be described as handsome, as he had a large head, red hair cut short, and a freckled fiery face, an indication of his hot temper. In his frenzies he would often chew the rushes off the floor. His voice was often harsh, and he normally spoke only Latin and French.

The most important event of the reign of Henry II concerning Westminster Abbey was the canonization of Edward the Confessor, which took place in 1161. Abbot Lawrence, a favourite of the King's, had been appointed Abbot of Westminster in 1158, and there is no doubt that he had used his influence with Pope Alexander III to effect the canonization of St

Edward. The Pope granted Abbot Lawrence, who came from St
Albans, the privilege of wearing the mitre, ring and gloves, but
he died in 1173 before they reached Westminster. King Henry
was certainly present at this ceremony, which took place on 7th
February.

Henry's reign was dominated to some extent by the quarrel
between himself and Thomas Becket, Archbishop of Canterbury.
Abbot Lawrence, however, wisely refrained from becoming
involved in this affair. Henry was far more interested in his
ancestral Abbey of Fontevrault in the valley of the Loire in
France near Saumur. There one can see the beautiful effigies of
Henry II and Eleanor of Aquitaine, both buried at Fontevrault,
united in death though they had been alienated during their lives.

Henry II was anxious that his son and heir Henry should be
crowned king during his lifetime in the Abbey Church of
Westminster, though Henry was destined to die before his father.
For this purpose King Henry obtained the consent of a general
assembly of his most important subjects at Windsor. This
ceremony took place in 1170 in Westminster Abbey, though the
bishops who took part in it were excommunicated by Thomas
Becket, Archbishop of Canterbury. There is an account of the
coronation banquet afterwards held in the Great Hall at
Westminster. For such an autocratic man as Henry II it seems
strange that he should humble himself by acting as a server. To
the sound of trumpets, with the trumpeters preceeding him, the
King brought up the boar's head as was the custom. His arrogant
son apparently did not appreciate the honours granted him.
When the Archbishop of York seated next to him remarked, "Be
glad, my good sonne, there is not another prince in the world
that hath such a server at his table", Henry replied, "Why doest
thou marvel at that? My father in doing it, thinketh it not more
than becometh him; he, being borne of princelie blood only on
the mother's side (Henry II's mother was the Empress Matilda,
only child of Henry I to survive him) serveth me that I am a born
prince, having both a King to my father, and a Queene to my
mother." This must be the only occasion when a reigning
English sovereign allowed his son to be crowned in his lifetime.

Henry II's third son Richard, who was at loggerheads with his
father from 1172 onwards, became King in 1189. Richard had

always supported his mother Eleanor of Aquitaine in her disputes with her husband. Richard Coeur de Lion is one of the great personalities in English history, a quixotic adventurer who dedicated his life to the Crusades. Every time we traverse the Houses of Parliament at Westminster, we see the heroic warrior King riding his horse and brandishing his sword. Yet in many ways Richard I was a bad king, neglecting his kingdom for the sake of an ideal. This Frenchman of mixed Norman and Angevin stock would willingly have sold London to raise money for the Crusades. There was much of the poet and the troubadour in his temperament, and like many of the Plantagenets he loved music. During his reign of nine and a half years, Richard only passed six months in England. Yet his coronation, which took place on 3rd September 1189, was very important, for there were a number of innovations. For instance, this is the first time we hear of the Bishop of Bath and Wells and the Bishop of Durham supporting the King. It is curious that 3rd September should be chosen, for the superstitious considered it a day of ill-omen. Early in the morning Richard was escorted from Westminster Palace by Baldwin, Archbishop of Canterbury, the Archbishops of Rouen, Dublin and Treves, and other clergy to the Abbey. The Archbishop of York was in a huff and did not appear. At the head of the procession moving to the high altar went the priors, next the abbots, followed by the bishops. Four barons carried four golden candelabra. Geoffrey de Lucy bore the King's Cap of Maintenance, William, Earl of Salisbury (one of Henry II's illegitimate sons) carried the rod topped by a dove, John, Earl of Mortmain and Gloucester the sword of state. William Marshal, Earl of Pembroke, bore the sceptre. The odious Prince John, younger brother of the new King, walked between two Earls. The honour of carrying the great golden crown was left to William de Mandeville, Earl of Essex, presumably supported by others, for it was very heavy.

One visualizes the beauty of St Edward's Westminster Abbey on this resplendent day, the chanting of the priests, and the tall, splendid King taking the Coronation Oath, kneeling before the high altar vowing that he would observe peace, honour and reverence towards God and exercise justice over all the people committed to his charge. It must be emphasized that the most sacred moments of the coronation were not the crowning, but the anointing ceremony by Baldwin, Archbishop of Canterbury – and so it remains through nine centuries of English history. All Richard's robes were stripped off, except his breeches and his shirt, so he was bare to the chest. The Archbishop then anointed him with holy oil on his head, chest and hands. This was the custom until Queen Victoria's coronation, who was only anointed on her head and hands. It was an innovation for Richard himself to take the crown from the altar and give it to the Archbishop, who reverently placed it on his head. Even for Richard it seemed so heavy that two Earls helped to take the weight. After the crowning the Te Deum was sung. There were two ominous incidents which slightly marred the ceremony. Men shuddered when a bat, while the day was yet light, fluttered about the Abbey and finally settled near the King's throne. It was considered an evil omen. Dean Stanley also relates that there was a sudden peal of bells at dusk, though the ministers at the Abbey had not agreed to it. Such incidents give an eerie impression of something almost supernatural.

At the banquet afterwards in Westminster Hall, Richard was magnificent, enjoying the merriment as he swayed on his seat, a powerfully built man, with his reddish gold hair, carefully trimmed beard and glaring blue eyes. This enigmatic man was always extremely fastidious in matters of dress. When, however, a deputation of Jews, who had been refused admittance to the Abbey, arrived at the Palace of Westminster with gifts for the King, the rabble, who hated them, rioted. This led to massacres in the city, which annoyed the King, especially on this day of his coronation. At the banquet the citizens of London served in the cellars, while the citizens of Winchester looked after the kitchens. Five years later, after his release from captivity, Richard was crowned again at Winchester, which was intended to placate his Saxon subjects.

Eminent historians have conflicting views of Richard's character. J.R. Green considered him "at heart a statesman, cool and patient in the execution of his plans as he was bold in their conception". Bishop Stubbs, however, wrote of him, "He was a very bad king ... his ambition was that of a mere warrior." Sir Winston Churchill too, in his *A History of the English-Speaking*

Peoples described him as, "a glorious paladin, whose life was one magnificent parade, which when ended left only an empty plain". Henry III, a vacillating monarch, extravagant, yet pious, left us the glory of the rebuilt Westminster Abbey and many other buildings. Although he was brave, and possessed noble ideals, what lasting benefits did Richard confer on us? Only a strange emptiness, and the pride in the achievements of "a splendid savage". The legend has outlived the man. Yet he should be judged by medieval standards, not by those of the twentieth century.

Fighting to the last, Richard died abroad in 1199, to be buried at his father's feet at Fontevrault. He was succeeded by his brother John, whose constant treachery against Richard had been generously forgiven. John had been his father's favourite, and Henry II had given him the nickname of John Lackland. He was a natural sceptic, and certainly a cynic, infamous enough but not so evil as he has been depicted, though guilty of murdering his nephew Arthur.

John was solemnly crowned by Hubert Walter, Archbishop of Canterbury, on Ascension Day, May 27th 1199. Walter had many misgivings both before and at the actual ceremony. He made the new King promise to uphold the peace of the land, to govern mercifully and fairly, to renounce "evil customs" and to be guided by the laws of Edward the Confessor. There is some evidence that the anointing spoon used at the coronation of King John is the same one used today for this part of the service. The ampulla − a vessel of fine gold − and the anointing spoon are the two oldest objects. The Abbey was hung with hundreds of yards of coloured cloth. Seventeen bishops, ten earls and many barons were present. The customary banquet was held in Westminster Hall when twenty-one fat oxen were roasted. John took the opportunity on this day to create Geoffrey Fitz Peter and William Marshall, Earls of Essex and Pembroke. Once again Geoffrey, Archbishop of York was not present, though the Bishop of Durham protested on his behalf that Hubert Walter had alone presided on this occasion. The five Barons of the Cinque Ports, because of their past services to the King, were permitted now and on future occasions to carry the canopy over the King in the procession to the Abbey, and to hold it over him when he was unclothed while the sacred ointment was applied to his body.

John managed to get rid of his first wife Isabel of Gloucester. By the summer of 1200 whilst on a tour of his continental dominions he fell madly in love with the beautiful daughter and heiress of Count Aymer of Angoulême, who was a mere child. Isabelle was already solemnly espoused to a baron, Hugh le Brun, Lord of Lusignan. By a cunning ruse John, with the aid of a Count Audemar, managed to abduct Isabelle from her father's house. John married the little girl whilst abroad. On returning to England, John, together with his bride, was crowned on 8th October 1200 in Westminster Abbey, by Hubert Walter. Almost £30 was spent on her royal robes. Eustice the chaplain, and Ambrose the clerk were each paid 25s. for singing the hymn "Christus Vicit" at her coronation. It was one of the Laudes and only performed before the King on the most solemn occasions. This child bride of John's, on whom he first doted, was also crowned in Canterbury Cathedral during Easter 1201.

John had more illegitimate children than his father Henry II, and was certainly unfaithful to Isabelle. The young Queen was reported to be adulterous. It is difficult to know whether or not to believe the story that John, after detecting her in an act of infidelity, had her lover hanged with the curtain rope above her bed. Isabelle was the mother of John's eldest son Henry, destined to be Westminster Abbey's greatest benefactor. If she was really so wanton as some of the medieval chroniclers, including Matthew Paris, assert, it is surprising that Hugh le Brun, Lord of Lusignan, was so willing after the death of his rival John, to marry the woman who had once been affianced to him. It suggests her strong sex appeal. They had several sons, including William de Valence, a half-brother of Henry III. His tomb in St Edmund's Chapel, Westminster Abbey, is the only existing example having Limoges champlevé enamel-work.

John took little interest in Westminster Abbey. His friend William de Humez, a Norman monk of Caen, succeeded Ralph Papillon as Abbot of Westminster in 1214, a year or two before the King's death. The King employed him as one of the pleni-potentiaries to negotiate for peace with France. John founded an abbey at Beaulieu, Hampshire. Although not a man of generous impulses, he was magnificent to the monks at Beaulieu. In his will John wished to be buried in the Church of the Blessed Virgin and St Wulfstan (a Saxon saint) at Worcester. So, today in order to see his tomb and the effigy surrounding it, it is necessary to travel to Worcester Cathedral.

Despite his grave defects of character, John possessed marked administrative ability, and in his constant peregrinations throughout England he learnt to know the country better than any of his predecessors. It was during his reign that the Exchequer officials rented houses in Westminster from the Abbot of Westminster. In such a way Westminster gradually became the administrative centre of the country.

BIBLIOGRAPHY

Annenberg, Walter, *Westminster Abbey* (1972)

Ashley, Maurice, *The Life and Times of William I* (1966)

Barlow, Frank, *Edward the Confessor* (1970)

Carpenter, Edward, (ed.) *A House of Kings* (1966)

Churchill, Winston, *A History of the English-Speaking Peoples* abridged by T. Baker (1964)

Dictionary of National Biography (Ed. Sir Sidney Lee) (1885)

Douglas, David C., *William the Conqueror* (1966)

Green, H.R., *A Short History of the English-Speaking People* Vols. I & II (1893)

Norgate, Kate, *Richard the Lion-Heart* (1924)

Noppen, J.G., *Royal Westminster and the Coronation* (1937)

Robinson, J. Armitage, *Gilbert Crispin Abbot of Westminster* A Study of the Abbey under Norman Rule (1911)

Saunders, Hilary St George, *Westminster Hall* (1951)

Stanley, Arthur Penrhyn, Dean of Westminster, *Historical Memorials of Westminster Abbey* (1869)

Warren, W.L., *Henry II* (1973)

Westlake, Herbert Francis, *The Church, Convent, Cathedral and College of St Peter, Westminster.* Vols I & II (1923)

Widmore, Richard, *History of Westminster Abbey* (1751)

2

Henry III and Westminster Abbey

The guides, who work so hard taking their large parties round the Abbey in the busy summer months, showing them the high altar and the exact position where our kings and queens have been crowned, very rarely mention that Henry III's coronation first took place in Gloucester Abbey. There was a good reason for this. The fortunes of England had sunk to a low pitch on Henry's accession in 1216. The Abbey was in the hands of Prince Louis of France, Shakespeare's 'Dauphin' in *King John*. Henry was aged only nine. Kate Norgate in her *The Minority of Henry III*, has described him as a child: "He had a beautiful face, with golden hair, and he was already noted for a gravity and dignity of speech beyond his years."

According to the contemporary historian Matthew Paris, a monk of St Albans Abbey, Henry was crowned by Bishops Peter of Winchester and Jocelyn of Bath. The Papal Legate Gualo sang the mass, but was tactful enough to let others take the principal part in the ceremony. Dean Stanley in his *Historical Memorials of Westminster Abbey* tells us that the full formalities were missing. Great care was, for instance, taken lest the rights of Canterbury should be infringed. The boy King was therefore crowned with a chaplet or garland rather than a crown. This incomplete coronation took place on 28th October 1216, the day of St Simon and St Jude. During the spring of 1220, Pope Honorius III ordered that owing to the irregularities of Henry's first crowning, a second coronation should take place in Westminster Abbey to be performed by Stephen Langton, Archbishop of Canterbury. Langton who was a great scholar and fine theologian had quarrelled with King John. He was fond of the young Henry.

It was arranged between the King and the new papal legate Pandulf that the ceremony should take place on Whit Sunday, 17th May. Henry had already conceived in his mind the wonderful project of rebuilding the Abbey Church of Westminster. It was on the eve of his coronation that he laid the first stone of the new Lady Chapel, on the site of the later Henry VII Chapel. For the last time a Plantagenet king was crowned in Edward the Confessor's church. In the nearby Tothill Fields, then a wild marshy district, were held "royal solemnities and goodly jousts". Tournaments were held in the Fields, including a grand one in 1226 at the coronation of Eleanor of Provence. Executions were sometimes carried out here. Perhaps the sunlight flickered on the face of the boy King – aged only thirteen – as he knelt before Stephen Langton and made his solemn vow to protect the Church of God and to preserve among other things the good laws of the realm. Many of the oldest nobles present rejoiced that Henry's coronation took place amidst such scenes of splendour when peace had been restored to the Kingdom.

It is timely to consider the character of Henry III. The new King was at heart an artist with an innate appreciation of beauty in all its forms, especially in art and architecture. He was devout rather than spiritually minded, and an important trait was his love of, and real feeling for tradition. These subtle influences had been fostered in his mind during the impressionable, formative years of his youth by Stephen Langton and others. Foreign travel, too, played a vital part in stimulating Henry. The inspiration of his life was his love and reverence for the Saxon King Edward the Confessor of blessed memory. Henry was immensely proud that he could trace his descent from King Alfred. It is true that Henry's predecessors had lived sometimes in Westminster Palace, but Henry regarded Westminster as his real home. He wanted to be near the Confessor's tomb, and his proximity to the Abbey made it easier for him to superintend the work of the royal masons. Two of his sons Edward and Edmund were given Anglo-Saxon names. The elder Edward, known sometimes as Edward of Westminster, because he was born at Westminster, was destined to be, perhaps, the greatest of our Plantagenet kings.

By heredity Henry might be a foreigner, but his character was moulded by the country which he ruled, and at times misruled. Matthew Paris has given us a description of Henry in his maturity. "He was of middling stature, and compact in body. The eyelid of one eye hung down, so as to hide some of the dark part of the eyeball. He possessed robust strength, and was inconsiderate in his acts, but as they generally came to fortunate and happy results, many thought that he was designated by the prophet Merlin, when speaking of the lynx, as penetrating everything with his eye." There was a naïve quality to Henry's mind, a kind of innocence which remained with him throughout his life.

The great day in the year for Henry was Edward the Confessor's Day, 13th October. Then the King was accustomed to gather round him the members of his household in their new robes, to knight the aspiring nobles, and to hold an imposing banquet.

Dr Stubbs, in his *Constitutional History of England* (Volume II) hardly gives a flattering character study of Henry. "Accomplished, refined, liberal, magnificent, rash rather than brave, impulsive and ambitious, pious, and in an ordinary sense virtuous, he was utterly devoid of all elements of greatness. The events of his reign brought out in fatal relief all his faults and weaknesses, making even such good points as he possessed contribute to establish the general conviction of his folly and falseness." He was querulous and suspicious and slow to forgive an injury. Henry was far more impressionable than his father John. John's heart was of millstone, Henry's of wax. Both were irresolute and oscillating. Yet he is hardly just when he states that Henry was utterly devoid of all elements of greatness. It is true that he had no pretensions to statesmanship, but he was great in a creative sense, especially in his rebuilding of Westminster Abbey. Henry's master passion was for building, and he devoted most of his energy to it sparing no expense, so that he has been accused of gross extravagance. Important work was undertaken at Westminster, Winchester, Windsor, Clarendon, Woodstock, Guildford, Gloucester, and Dublin Castle during his reign.

Henry's inspiration owed much to his travels in France, where he stayed throughout 1242 and until the end of September during

The nave of Westminster Abbey, looking west from the organ loft.

The tomb of Henry III from the North Ambulatory

the following year. The King had special opportunities of studying the noble works of architecture, which were being erected in France. The resemblance between Reims and Westminster Abbey has been mentioned often enough, and the choir of the new church at Reims had been completed and consecrated as early as 1241. At the time when the exquisite chapter house in Westminster Abbey was being planned during 1245-1249, the Sainte-Chapelle in Paris was being built. There is no doubt that the carving and tracery in the Sainte-Chapelle influenced the work in Henry III's chapter house. During his various visits to Amiens, especially from 1248 onwards, Henry was able to inspect the progress being undertaken in the building of the choir of this beautiful cathedral. The north front and portals of Westminster Abbey were being erected just after the west front at Amiens had been completed. It is no accident therefore that there is a resemblance between Westminster Abbey and Amiens Cathedral.

Another strong impulse in Henry's mind may have owed its origin to the rebuilding of the Abbey of St Denys by the contemporary French King Louis IX. It is possible that it suggested to Henry the idea of making Westminster a royal burial place for himself and his descendants. King Louis was critical of Henry that he attended three masses a day, telling him that he ought to hear sermons, as well as attend Mass. It made no difference to Henry. There was much of the monk in him. Whilst in France he preferred to live in a monastery rather than in a palace.

To rebuild Westminster Abbey it was mostly necessary to demolish Edward the Confessor's Church, and the work involved was naturally tremendous. Today we marvel at the austere Gothic beauty of the Abbey, not mindful of or appreciative of the problems facing the 800 workmen engaged on it under the royal master mason. Besides those engaged on the great work, there were the quarry-men who dug out the stone in Caen in Normandy, Purbeck in Dorset and other places. There were the seamen, who transported it across the Channel, and the wagoners, who struggled with their vital loads of material along roads full of ruts to Westminster. Meanwhile in the forests of England there was the resounding crash of oaks as the woodmen felled trees to be borne to Westminster as timber. As early as 1234 King Henry had given twenty oaks to be used for the building of the Lady Chapel from the forest of Tonbridge. Merchants, too, played their part in collecting the materials for work in cloth and jewellery, in mosaic and metal, so loved by the King and his father. Tilers used their specialized skill at Chertsea and elsewhere. Then there were the financiers, who were required to advance money for the wages of those engaged in the undertaking.

The rebuilding of Westminster Abbey must not be considered as an isolated activity. The west front of Wells Cathedral in Somerset had lately been consecrated, while the building of the beautiful Cistercian Abbey of Tintern, now a noble ruin, had already begun. The choir of the Temple Church was hallowed in 1240.

The most famous of King Henry's master masons was surely Master Henry, who had held this office since 1243. Herbert Francis Westlake in his scholarly volumes on Westminster Abbey, maintains that Master Henry de Reyns, as he is sometimes styled, was a foreigner coming from Reims. This contention has been disputed, partly on the grounds that the name de Reyne, or similar variations, is common enough in Rayne in the County of Essex, which lies just north of the road between Bishop's Stortford and Coggeshall. Henry III is known to have stayed there for several days in August 1238. The opinion of the experts today inclines to the view that Master Henry was an Englishman.

The King closely superintended the work of the rebuilding of Westminster Abbey, and his intimate relations with his various master masons, both in the Church and in the Palace must be stressed. Gifts of wine often passed between Henry and his master masons. In Westminster Palace during 1236-1237 the Keeper of the Works was John of Waverley, and two years later Master Alexander was the chief carpenter.

According to the Westminster Abbey accounts, Master Alexander was paid £106. 13s. 4d. for providing timber, and he worked on the spire of the belfry. Master Henry, the Master Mason is also mentioned in the accounts. On one occasion during the fifth year of the rebuilding, he was paid 40 marks, the equivalent of £26. 13s. 4d. for task-work (known today as piece-work). During the seventh year Peter the Spaniard, a painter, was a special favourite of Henry III, and other foreigners were employed in the Abbey.

The Master Mason, Henry de Reyns, lived in a house near the Abbey, from where he could easily supervise the army of workmen in the Abbey. By 1254-1255 he had been succeeded by Master John of Gloucester, who was promised parcels of land for his services to the King at Westminster, Woodstock, Gloucester and elsewhere. He was also favoured by the grant of all tolls and tollage for life: like Master Henry, he lived in a house and curtilage in Westminster with his wife Alice and son named Edward.

The King was eager that the Abbey should be made more resplendent by gold statues and other beautiful works of art. Here is one example of his munificence.

> The King to the treasurer and chamberlains, Greeting. Deliver from our Treasury to Edward, son of Odo 25 marks and 4d., for pure gold bought at our command, weighing 30s. 4d to make two statues to be offered at the Shrine of St Edward, and to the same Edward 54s. 6d. for precious stones bought for the same statues and for his work on them, and to the same Edward 24s. 3d, for silver gilt bought and placed about them, and for work on that silver, and to the same 67s. 1d. for a silver candlestick bought and offered there, weighing 55s. 7d. with gold work thereon ... .

Henry was very keen on the interior decoration of his palaces. He commanded Edward, son of Odo, Keeper of the King's works at Westminster, to see that the fireplace to the Queen's chamber there be made higher, and cause it to be painted and portrayed on the said fireplace a figure of winter, made the more like winter by its sad countenance and other miserable attitudes of the body.

The queen referred to was Eleanor of Provence, one of the five beautiful daughters of Berenger, Count of Provence, the grandson of Alfonso, King of Aragon. Eleanor, who was to acquire quite an ascendancy over the mind of her husband, was scarcely fourteen when she married Henry in Canterbury Cathedral during January 1236. Her coronation in Westminster Abbey, described by Matthew Paris, was a splendid affair. He wrote: "But why need I recount the train of those who performed the offices of the church? Why describe the profusion of dishes which furnished the table, the abundance of venison, the variety of fish, the diversity of wine, the gaiety of the Jugglers, the comeliness of the attendants?" The Barons of the Cinque Ports carried the canopy over the Queen's head. Henry, who had extravagant tastes and was a great fop, wore a robe of resplendent gold consisting of materials called baudekins, according to Matthew Paris. The citizens of London headed by their Mayor, Andrew Buckerel "everie man bearing gold or silver cups in their hands", according to Stow, mounted on horses, escorted the King from the Tower to the Abbey. At the banquet after the coronation held in Westminster Hall, they claimed the privilege of serving as cellarers, handing the wine to the royal butler. The banquet was somewhat marred by the absence of the Chief Butler, Hugh de Albini, who had incurred the enmity of the Archbishop of Canterbury and been excommunicated by him for refusing to let him hunt in his Sussex forest.

The Londoners hated Queen Eleanor because they considered her arrogant, disliked her foreign favourites and the influence she had acquired over her husband. On one occasion when she was travelling from the Tower by boat on the Thames to London Bridge, intending to go to Windsor, they abused her with foul words, even hurling stones at her. Henry was uxorious, and so far as is known faithful to Eleanor. Eleanor's sister Sanchia of Provence, third daughter of Raymond Berenger, Count of Provence, married the King's younger brother Richard of Cornwall (afterwards King of the Romans) in the Abbey of Westminster on 22nd November 1243, according to Westlake and the *Complete Peerage* Volume III. Sandford, in a *Genealogical History of the Kings of England*, however, makes no mention of Westminster as the setting for the wedding. Townsend, the Windsor herald, states that the marriage of Richard of Cornwall — it was his second marriage — and Sanchia took place at Westminster during the feast of St Cecilia (a Sunday). If we accept Westlake's statement, and the matter is open to doubt, this is the first marriage to take place in Henry's newly consecrated

church, for Aveline and Edmund Crouchback were only united
in marriage in 1269.

Many foreigners, especially Italians, accompanied the young
Eleanor to England, among them her uncle Peter of Savoy,
known as such because the Queen persuaded Henry to give him
valuable property in the part of London known as 'The Savoy'.
There Peter had a splendid palace built for himself, which
Eleanor later bought from him, so as to hand it over as a gift to
her younger son Edmund Earl of Lancaster, nicknamed Edmund
Crouchback. The Londoners groaned under excessive taxation
and criticized the royal couple for their extravagance.

Henry resorted to all kinds of subterfuges for the purpose of
raising sufficient funds for the rebuilding of Westminster Abbey.
The Jews were bled handsomely. The reluctant citizens were
persuaded to make Henry valuable new year's gifts. The
treasurer and barons of the Exchequer in 1254 received royal
commands to donate 3,000 marks annually towards the extension
of the work, a measure which hardly endeared Henry to the
barons. About five years earlier the Sheriff of Kent received the
royal command to instruct all persons having grey stone for sale
to have it borne to Westminster. An eighteenth-century historian
Widmore quoted a report that the total cost of the works up to
1260-1261 was nearly £30,000. Henry's relations with two of the
Abbots of Westminster were intimate, and both Richard de
Crockesley, and Richard de Ware, who succeeded de
Crockesley,[1] were men of ability. Matthew of Westminster tells
us that Crockesley was authorized to celebrate mass like a pontiff,
and that he dedicated the Chapel of St Edmund near the north
door of the Abbey. It is recorded that Henry presented him with
ten deer and three casks of wine for the feast of St Edward.
According to Matthew Paris, Crockesley was handsome, a fluent
speaker and learned in the Civil and Canon Law. Henry
frequently employed him on important foreign missions to
Germany, Italy and elsewhere. He once travelled to Gascony
with a monk named Normannus to hand over the Virgin's girdle
to Henry III and his Queen. Henry's friend Crockesley died in

[1] Westlake states that Philip de Lewesham succeeded Crockesley as Abbot-elect, but
died almost immediately.

1258 after twelve years as Abbot and is now buried in the Chapel of St Nicholas in the Abbey.

Abbot de Ware is chiefly celebrated for his mission to Rome to bring back the workmen and porphyries for fashioning the exquisite Cosmati pavement and other work of delicate mosaic, a rare gem which is one of the Abbey's most cherished possessions. So precious is it that a carpet is usually spread over most of it to protect it. Only the pavement remains today in the sanctuary. The name of the chief artist was Peter, a Roman citizen and the material used was Purbeck marble.

Richard de Ware possessed remarkable negotiating ability. We first hear of him as proctor to Abbot Crockesley in June 1257. Appointed a papal chaplain two years later, he was authorized to borrow 1,000 marks for promoting the business of the Abbey both in Rome and in Florence where he borrowed from merchants. While de Ware was Abbot, Henry was forced by his embarrassing debts to ask for the temporary handing over to him of gold, precious stones and jewels belong to the Confessor's Shrine. The King gave his solemn oath that he would restore them to the monastery within sixteen months, and he kept his word. According to the Abbey muniments (Mun. 9464) they were all returned, on 1st June 1267.

It is not without interest to mention some of the King's personal tastes. He was very fond of fish, which was just as well owing not only to Friday abstinence from eating meat, but because meat was very scarce during the winter months in the Middle Ages. However, the Lenten diet of fish sometimes became monotonous to Henry and Eleanor, and orders were therefore given to the Sheriff of Gloucester to purchase as many lampreys as possible in his bailiwick. John of Sandon, the King's cook, was entrusted with the duty of travelling to Gloucester to obtain these lampreys. Both King and Queen were very partial to them, and preferred them cooked in bread and jelly. Other favourites were herrings, and the Sheriff of Norfolk took care to provide for Henry only the most "exquisite" herrings. Salmon pasties especially made for him sound a great delicacy, and the King was very fond of them. In the Tower of London Henry III kept several wild animals, including an elephant, which was a present from Louis IX of France, and also a lion. William, keeper of the lion, was entitled to 14s., which he spent on buying chains and other things for the use of the beasts.

Henry III was responsible for the building of the eastern portion of Westminster Abbey. Today we marvel at its beauty, grateful that important parts were erected during the middle and later thirteenth century when Gothic architecture was at its best. It is fortunate that the later builders held fast to the ideals nourished by the early pioneers. In its great height in relation to its width, especially at the eastern end, we are reminded of the cathedrals of northern France, of Amiens, Rheims or Rouen. Evidence of the French influence on mainly English work is very striking.

One of the chief glories of Henry III's rebuilt Westminster Abbey was the chapter house, "incomparable" as it was described by Matthew of Paris. If Henry's spirit still haunts the environs of Westminster Abbey, it is here that he might feel most at home. The chapter house was begun in 1250, and completed in 1253. An English mason, Master Alberic was employed on the work under the direction of Master Henry. The chapter house is remarkable for several reasons. Except for Lincoln, it is the largest chapter house in England. It is the only example, except for Worcester, of a round or octagonal chapter house instead of the rectangular or longitudinal buildings attached to Benedictine monasteries. Outside the chapter house were some of the earliest tombs. Henry III's Abbot Ware defined the original purpose of the chapter house, mentioned by Dean Stanley, "It is 'the Little House', in which the convent meets to consult for its welfare." Disputes were decided by the Abbots and his Council. Here the monks made their confessions, and were punished for violating the rules of the Benedictine order. The penalties were harsh, for the older monks were sometimes flogged in public. It was the custom for the monks to walk in double file in a procession from the church to the chapter house after Mass at about 9 a.m. The chapter house, however, was used for other important purposes, for instance for meetings of the King's Council on 26th March 1257. During the reign of Henry III's son, who succeeded him as Edward I, it served as the place where the House of Commons held their sessions. It was in the chapter house, too, where the principal ceremonial events were planned, today organized in the Jerusalem Chamber.

No King has been fonder of great ceremonial occasions than Henry III. It was on St Edward the Confessor's day, 13th October 1269, that the King – now an old man – together with his sons Edward and Edmund and with his brothers, carried on their shoulders the relics of the saint to the new shrine behind the high altar. A most important day in the Abbey's history, and it was on this occasion that the monks of Westminster celebrated Mass in the new building for the first time. Queen Eleanor offered jewels of great value at the shrine.

Matthew Paris gives an account of how St Edward's Day was celebrated in 1247. The King had just received from the East a portion of the holy blood. Dressed in humble raiment, Henry bore the precious vase containing this relic all the way from St Paul's to the Abbey, on foot. Through the Abbey buildings moved Henry, heading an imposing procession, and into the church. It was so crowded that a man could hardly move. The Bishop of Norwich celebrated Mass and preached the sermon.

The Plantagenet kings were sometimes at loggerheads with their sons, but a strong affection existed between Henry III and his sons Edward and Edmund. We can picture Edward as a boy of fourteen saying his tearful farewell to his father at Portsmouth as the King was about to sail for Gascony. Intriguing nobles, however, managed to persuade Henry on one occasion that Edward was plotting to dethrone him, together with Earl Simon de Montford. There was no truth in these insinuations, but Henry refused to see Edward, though he said in his emotional way: "Do not let my son Edward appear before me, for if I see him I shall not be able to refrain myself from kissing him." They were soon reconciled.

Edward of Westminster was a magnificent figure of a man, tall, broad-chested, with the long, nervous arms of a swordsman. He was handsome, but he apparently inherited from his father a peculiar droop of the left eyelid. He was a fluent and persuasive speaker, though his voice was often indistinct. Edward was able to speak English eloquently as well as French and Latin. In many ways he might be compared with Alfred the Great. During his

early life in 1254 Edward visited Spain where he was knighted by
Alfonso X of Castile at Burgos, and during October was married
to Alfonso's half-sister Eleanor (half-Spanish by birth) at the
monastery church of Las Huelgas. Eleanor of Castile was to
acquire an ardent love for Westminster and for the Abbey. On
the whole England has been fortunate in the consorts of her
Plantagenet kings, Edward I and Edward III. Both Eleanor of
Castile and Philippa of Hainault were outstanding women.
Edward of Westminster later fought with great bravery in the
Crusades where he was joined in Palestine by his younger
brother Edmund during 1271.

Edmund, gay and affable by temperament and very generous
was very popular with his men, according to Matthew Paris.
Like his father, he was religious. He was nicknamed Crouchback
(or Crossedback) because of his connection with the Crusades.
Created Earl of Lancaster in 1267, Henry III accepted on his son's
behalf the offer of Pope Alexander IV in 1255, to invest Edmund
with the Kingdom of Sicily and Apulia, and he was actually
styled King of Sicily. This grant of the Sicilian crown was,
however, ultimately cancelled. Edmund Crouchback's
connection with Westminster Abbey is very intimate, for Henry
married his younger son to an important and beautiful heiress,
Aveline de Forz, daughter of William Earl of Albemarle, who
owned vast estates in Devon and elsewhere. She was also the
heiress to her mother's inheritance. It is a little uncertain whether
this marriage is the first recorded one to take place in Henry III's
rebuilt church in 1270. Unfortunately Aveline died early, and
Edmund then married Blanche, widow of Henry King of
Navarre, and daughter of Robert, Count of Artois. How fitting
it is that Edmund and Aveline should both be buried in
Westminster Abbey, and their tombs on the north of the High
Altar are two of the finest medieval tombs in the whole building.
They are separated only by the resplendent tomb of Aymer de
Valence, Earl of Pembroke, and more of him anon. The richly
decorated triple canopy over the tomb of Edmund Crouchback
has been attributed to Master Alexander of Abingdon. There is
his beautifully sculptured effigy. His hands are folded and he is in
an attitude of prayer.

Three of Henry III's children, Katherine, Richard and John,

who died in infancy, are buried in Westminster Abbey. Katherine died in 1257 aged five and was buried under a segmental arch between the chapels of St Edmund and St Benedict. One is impressed with the intimate connection of Henry's family with the Abbey he created. His younger brother Richard, Earl of Cornwall, elected King of the Romans, certainly visited the Abbey many times, together with his wife Sanchia.

One of Henry's celebrated master masons was Robert of Beverley. In 1263, together with Master Odo the carpenter, Master Robert was engrossed in repairing Westminster Palace after a fire. Master Robert, too, was regularly employed in the Abbey. Abbot Richard de Ware's Book of Customs mentions a present from the Convent to a goldsmith Master R. de Frenlingham, possibly the Abbey plumber, and one to Master Robert de Beverley. He also received a payment for life from Henry III during 1272 – the year the King died.

He was sixty-five, and his long reign had extended over a period of fifty-six years. As unconsciousness gradually stole over his failing senses when he lay dying in his Palace of Westminster on St Edmund's Day, 16th November, he may have been disturbed by the rude cries of the tumultuous Londoners, who had given him so much trouble during his life. Sir F.M. Powicke aptly wrote of Henry in the second volume of his work, *King Henry III and the Lord Edward*: "Henry had rarely found the peace for which his nature must have craved ... yet he had held his own, with the uneasy persistence and the reluctant submission to hard facts of the querulous realist ... yet the old man left his Kingdom greater than it was when a fair-faced child, he rode from Devizes to be crowned at Gloucester. England was more united, more prosperous, more richly endowed, more beautiful in 1272 than it was in 1216."

Such was the reverence of the old King for the memory of Edward the Confessor, that he had expressed a desire that his mortal remains should be placed in the old coffin in which that Saxon king had originally been interred. Henry was also extremely attached to the Abbey of Fontevrault in the valley of the Loire where several of our kings and queens were buried, including his own mother Isabelle of Angoulême, Henry II and Eleanor of Aquitaine, and their son Richard I. As a result of this deep sentiment his heart was taken across the seas to Fontevrault to be buried there. Henry had in his earlier life promised that his heart should be deposited in this ancestral burial-place, and the Abbess of Fontevrault — a grand lady in her own right — now claimed fulfilment of the promise.

Henry III was given a magnificent funeral at Westminster Abbey. His gilt-bronze effigy, the work of an artist, William Torel, a London goldsmith, was not completed until 1291. Edward was absent from the Kingdom on his father's death, but he later brought back precious and exquisite stones of jasper to beautify the tomb.

BIBLIOGRAPHY

Harvey, John, *The Plantagenets* (1971 edition)
Lethaby, W.R., *Westminster Abbey and the Kings' Craftsmen. A Study of Medieval buildings* (1931)
  Westminster Abbey Re-examined (1925)
Neale J. and Brayley E. *History and Antiquities of the Abbey Church of St Peter, Westminster* 2 Vols. 1818
Norgate, Kate, *John Lackland* (1902) *The Minority of Henry III*
Paris, Matthew, Chronicles of, *English History 1235-1273*. Tr. J.A. Giles
Powicke, Sir F.M., *Henry III and the Lord Edward* Vols. 1 and 2 (1947)
Sandford, Francis, *Genealogical History of the Kings of England*
Stanley, Arthur Penrhyn, *Historical Memorials of Westminster Abbey*
Stubbs, W.S. Dr, *Constitutional History of England in its History & Development, 1875-1878*
Vaughan, Richard, *Matthew Paris* (1958)
Warron, W.L., *King John* (1961)

3

Edward I and his Successors

Edward was in Messina in Sicily when he heard of his father's death. Although the prince had recently lost one of his infant sons, he was more grief-stricken by Henry III's decease. His uncle, Charles of Anjou, asked him how it was possible to bear the loss of his son in such a resigned way, yet to succumb to grief for the death of an old man. Edward replied that he might have other sons, but he could never replace his father. On his return journey to England, Edward received a triumphal reception in Rome, Padua and Milan where he was given a present of some fine horses caparisoned in scarlet trappings.

Edward, who had been proclaimed King during his absence abroad, landed at Dover on 2nd August 1274 together with his beloved first Queen Eleanor of Castile. They were crowned together on 19th August in Westminster Abbey – the first to be jointly crowned there – by the Archbishop of Canterbury, Kilwardby. The coronation banquet was held in Westminster Hall. 440 oxen and cows, 430 sheep, 450 pigs and 6 fat boars had to be slaughtered to provide suitable fare for this great occasion. Edward I's coronation was especially memorable because of the presence of Alexander III King of Scotland, who attended the banquet "with a hundred knights on horseback who, as soon as they dismounted turned their steeds loose for anyone to catch and keep that thought proper". Alexander's armorial bearings were hung in the choir of Westminster Abbey, but he was compelled to pay homage to the new King. Llewellyn, Prince of North Wales, however, refused to render homage to Edward, despite his peremptory demand. During the two following years he refused to obey the royal summons, but was forced to make his submission in 1276 and perform the homage.

According to Dean Stanley, Edward I was the first sovereign to discontinue the commemoration of the event in wearing the crown at the three festivals, Christmas, Easter and Whitsun. Edward was not so attached to Westminster Palace or to the Abbey as his father had been, though the King and Queen regularly resided there up to Eleanor's death in November 1290. He may then have conceived a dislike for the place, and rarely stayed there. Richard de Ware, the Abbot of Westminster, who had given Henry III splendid service, stood high in Edward's favour. For instance in 1278 when various of the great monasteries of England were deprived of their ancient liberties, those of Westminster Abbey were restored after their formal surrender. Richard de Ware died towards the end of 1283 ("about St Andrew's Day") and was succeeded by Walter de Wenlock, destined to be one of Westminster Abbey's outstanding abbots. He became treasurer to Queen Eleanor of Castile and took charge of her various benefactions to the Abbey. It is evident that Wenlock enjoyed the patronage and friendship of Edward I, perhaps the greatest of the Plantagenet kings. There is no doubt whatsoever that he was a fine statesman having learnt his craft the hard way as his father's heir.

Edward was quick to take offence, humorous and usually affable, but he was hot-tempered, like most of the Plantagenets. Together with Queen Eleanor he attended the marriage of their third daughter Margaret in Westminster Abbey. She married John, the second Duke of Brabant. For some reason, which is not clear, Edward lost his temper with one of his esquires, giving him a sharp rap with his wand without just cause. Agnes Strickland in her account of the life of Eleanor of Castile, relates that Edward paid the man £13. 6s. 8d. as compensation and was generous enough to admit that he was in the wrong.

Edward I's wardrobe book 1296-97 also contains evidence of the King's violent temper. "To Adam the King's goldsmith for a great ruby and a great emerald bought to set in a certain coronet of the Countess of Holland, the King's daughter, in place of the two stones which were lost when the King threw the coronet in the fire at Ipswich." The wardrobe book has quaint allusions to journeys undertaken by Margaret Duchess of Brabant. Richard de Goseford, Master of the Swan of Yarmouth going from thence to Harwich for the Passage of Lady Margaret Duchess of Brabant towards Brabant for the wages of 1 constable at 6d. per day and 53 seamen at 3d. per day.

Edward I was the founder of our parliamentary system. At a great parliament held at Westminster on 22nd April 1275, the King by the assent of his hereditary peers and of all the commonality of the land, proclaimed "the Statute of Westminster", a body of fifty-one chapters of law. By temperament he was therefore a law-giver, and he employed Francesco Accursi, the son of the famous legist of Bologna in his service.

Edward was fortunate on the whole, both as prince and King. Nicholas Trevet, son of a Somerset knight, relates that when Edward was quite young he was playing chess with a knight in a vaulted chamber. For some inexplicable reason Edward suddenly rose from his chair and left the room just before an enormous stone fell on the spot where he had been sitting. On another occasion when his horse slipped at Winchelsea, he was nearly crushed to death, but escaped as if by a miracle.

This able man and strong ruler, a noble character, had many intimate associations with the Abbey. To his contemporaries he was Edward 'Longshanks' and the 'Hammer of the Scots'. He was responsible for the magnificent tombs erected to commemorate his father Henry III and his wife Eleanor of Castile. It was Edward's son, Prince Alfonso, when only a boy, who hung the golden coronet of Llewellyn, last native Prince of Wales, before St Edward's Shrine. Prince Alfonso died soon afterwards and was buried near the saint after whom his father had been named.

All visitors to Westminster Abbey ask to see the celebrated Stone of Scone, which was, as it is well known, seized in 1297 by Edward, and transported from Scotland to Westminster Abbey where it was placed in the Abbot's custody. The Scots deeply reverenced the Stone of Scone on which their Kings had been crowned for centuries. Edward commissioned Walter of Durham to construct a chair of wood, although he had originally intended it to be of bronze. Master Walter was at the same time busy working on the Painted Chamber in Westminster Palace and probably on the chapter house. Master Walter was responsible for the decoration of the chair, and the historic Stone of Scone formed part of the fabric of the oak chair. Seated thereon, all our Kings have been crowned with the exception of two. Edward I's son, who succeeded him as Edward II, was the first King to sit on the chair for his coronation in 1308. It is unfortunate that much of its beauty has been altogether ruined by the repellent habit of schoolboys and others during the eighteenth century who had their names and initials carved on it. How much more elegant and beautiful is the fifteenth-century screen erected in 1441 depicting scenes from the life of Edward the Confessor.

Edward was a good judge of character, and hard to deceive. On one occasion he found his mother, Eleanor of Provence, who lived much at Amesbury after the death of Henry III, in a state of excitement. She declared that a man had told her that he had been cured of blindness while presumably praying at the tomb of Henry III in Westminster Abbey. Edward incurred his mother's wrath by telling her that the man was lying. She told him to leave the room as if he was a small boy. Trevet records that Edward remarked: "I know enough of my father's justice to be sure that he would rather have torn out the eyes of this rascal when they were sound than have given sight to such a rascal."

Edward's married life with Eleanor of Castile, his first wife, was extremely happy, and their union lasted thirty-six years. When her husband tried to dissuade her from accompanying him on his crusades she proudly said: "The way to heaven is as near from Palestine as from England." In the autumn of 1290 she was suddenly taken ill near Grantham in Lincolnshire before she could join her husband in Scotland. Her wardrobe book mentions the payment of one mark to Henry of Montpelier for syrup and other medicines bought at Lincoln. She died on 29th November in Nottinghamshire aged forty-six. Agnes Strickland gives an account of the melancholy progress of her funeral from Grantham to Westminster. How the royal bier was placed in some central part of a town, and indeed before the high altar of the churches. In memory of the "chère reine", as he called her, Edward erected crosses. Today only three memorial crosses remain, those at Northampton, Geddington and Waltham. The one at Charing Cross[1] is a replica of the original cross. So this great Queen was given a magnificent funeral in Westminster Abbey. The service was conducted by the Bishop of Lincoln, because the Archbishop of Canterbury was at loggerheads with Walter de Wenlock the Abbot of Westminster.

It was William Torel who cast the beautiful bronze effigy of Henry III's daughter-in-law, Eleanor of Castile in 1291, perhaps one of the loveliest Gothic sculptures in the Abbey. There she lies, serene in death as she was so often in life, her hair falling over her shoulders. So as to cast the Queen's statue, Torel built his furnace in St Margaret's Churchyard. Two other similar images of Eleanor once existed at Blackfriars Monastery where her heart was buried, and at Lincoln. The goldsmith Torel is reputed to have received £113. 6s. 8d. for the three works. The exquisite carved iron grille familiar to those who know the Abbey, is the work of Master Thomas of Leighton. The executors of Eleanor of Castile's will record in 1295 payments to "Master Thomas of Leightone, smith for making ironwork round the tomb of the Queen at Westminster." Thomas was actually paid £12 for this work and for its carriage from Leighton as far as Westminster. It included his expenses and those of his workmen whilst in London.

Fabyan related that two wax tapers were kept burning upon her tomb both day and night, "which hath so continued syn the day of her burying to this present". She is said to have introduced the fashion for hanging tapestries and carpets on walls.

Edward I survived his first Queen by sixteen years, dying at Burgh-on-the-Sands on 7th July 1307, whilst on the way to Scotland. For sixteen weeks his body lay in Waltham Abbey, by the grave of Harold II. Edward was buried on St Simon and St Jude's Day 28th October, in Westminster Abbey. It was Anthony Bek, Bishop of Durham and Titular Patriarch of Jerusalem, high in favour with Edward II, although he had quarrelled with his father, who was given the honour of

---

[1] Eleanor is the "chère reine" from which it is said Charing Cross derives its name. But the name may come from "char rynge" which was a ring or parking place for horses when the owners attended levees or had business at Westminster.

A detail from the north side of the monument to Edmund Crouchback,
Earl of Lancaster

The tomb effigy of Henry III by William Torel

The tomb of Cardinal Simon Langham, Abbot of Westminster by
Henry Yevele

guarding Edward's body and conducting the funeral service. Edward lies near the tomb of his much loved father. The words Malleus Scotorum, "the Hammer or Crusher of the Scots" are inscribed on Edward of Westminster's tomb.

The tragedy of Edward of Caernarvon's life was that he was absolutely unsuited to the position of King, when he inherited from his father. There had been serious quarrels between Edward and his son. During the summer of 1305, Edward I had banished him from Court for insulting his chief minister, although there was later a reconciliation. The King himself knighted his son in the chapel of the Palace of Westminster and he granted him the Duchy of Aquitaine and other duchies. At an important ceremony in May 1306 in the Abbey at Westminster, Prince Edward knighted several hundred candidates. There followed a splendid banquet, during which eighty minstrels played to the distinguished company. Royal swan was one of the dishes served.

Yet the King's last days were saddened by his anxiety concerning Edward's intimate friendship with Peter of Gaveston ("Perrot de Gaveston"), whose father came from a Gascon village and was of ancient stock. Edward I, with a father's insight, feared that the young Prince was indulging in a homosexual affair with Gaveston, who "loved his son inordinately", according to the contemporary chronicles. Such evidence as we have would indicate very strongly that Edward II was a homosexual, although perhaps it would be more correct to call him a heterosexual, for he was later to father sons, including the one who would prove outstanding, Edward III. One chronicler, Guisborough mentions that when the Prince asked the Earldom of Cornwall for Gaveston, Edward I knocked him down and kicked him. Gaveston was temporarily banished the Kingdom and was only recalled after the death of Edward I.

On 25th January 1308, the new King Edward II was married in France to the Princess Isabella, daughter of Philip IV of France, the "She-Wolf of France" as she is called, one of the most depraved of our medieval Queen Consorts, even if provoked to evil deeds. Edward and Isabella were both crowned together on 25th February in Westminster Abbey. It was a splendid ceremony. In the procession to the Abbey the two golden spurs were borne by Aymer de Valence, Earl of Pembroke, a soldier and a statesman frequently employed by Edward I and his son on diplomatic missions. Aymer was followed by the Earl of Hereford, bearing the royal sceptre with the cross, then came Henry of Lancaster, son of Edmund Crouchback the King's great-uncle carrying the royal staff with a dove on the top. Much to the rage and envy of the barons, Gaveston, now Earl of Cornwall, walked immediately in front of the King carrying the Sword of St Edward and the crown decorated and sparkling with precious stones. As was customary the canopy over the King's head was supported by the Barons of the Cinque Ports. So they moved to the high altar where Edward and his French Queen were crowned by Henry Woodlock, Bishop of Winchester, who officiated in the place of Robert Winchelsey, Archbishop of Canterbury. He was ill and absent in Rome. The choice of Woodlock was an insult to the memory of Edward I, for he had conspired against him.

It is probable that Edward II made his royal oaths in French and not in Latin, because he wanted his audience in the Abbey to understand what was transpiring. In any case French was the mother tongue of most people present. Bishop Woodlock questioned Edward concerning the four parts of the coronation oath. One of the questions seemed to take a new form: "Will you consent to hold and keep the laws and righteous customs which the community of your realm shall have chosen, and will you defend them and strengthen them to the honour of God, to the utmost of your power?" This seemed to imply that the people of the Kingdom, through their representatives in Parliament, were entitled to control by counsel and consent the legislative action and policy of the King.

Dean Stanley relates that the clergy of the Abbey were well satisfied when Sir John Bakewell, an old enemy of the monastery, was trodden to death.

At the coronation banquet, Gaveston infuriated the barons by wearing royal purple instead of cloth of gold. The King's wanton affection for his arrogant favourite was manifest to everybody. They could hardly stomach their fury when Edward called Gaveston "his brother Perrot". The banquet was hardly a success because the food was badly cooked. There were many French princes and nobles present, and they sent exasperated accounts home concerning the insults their Queen had been subjected to. She herself complained to her father about Gaveston's behaviour. The favourite's waspish wit and quick sallies infuriated the English barons. Gaveston had nicknames for all of them. Aymer de Valence, Earl of Pembroke, who was dark, thin and sallow-complexioned was called "Joseph the Jew", Guy de Beauchamp, Earl of Warwick "the Wild Boar of Ardenne" because he foamed at the mouth when angry, and Henry, Earl of Lancaster "the Stage Player".

The barons were so much aggrieved by Gaveston being allowed to walk in the procession immediately before the King, "without regard to the claims of inheritance, or the precedent of former reigns", that they met together three days afterwards in the refectory of the monks at Westminster, and petitioned the King that his foreign favourite should be banished.

Edward of Caernarvon, a tall handsome man, was suited by temperament to be a country squire, and he had many cultured tastes. He was fond of the theatre, an amateur poet, and he had an even stronger sense of humour than his father. Once when Jack of St Albans, the royal painter, danced on a table before the King, he amused Edward so much "making him laugh beyond measure" that he gave the fellow 50s. from his own hand. He was a curious character, liking to play cross and pile (pitch and toss) with Henry his barber and on one occasion lost 5s. to him. He was, too, of exceptional bodily strength. As Harold F. Hutchinson states in his *Edward II The Pliant King*, Marlowe in his great play was more alive to the poetry and tragedy of homosexuality and consequently understood Edward's character better than most subsequent historians.

Walter de Wenlock, Abbot of Westminster, who had enjoyed the confidence of Edward I, took good care to cultivate friendly relations with Prince Edward – the Prince of Wales – during his father's lifetime. For instance he paid the Prince's clerk as much as £6. 13s. 4d. for a horse intended to be for his own use. Perhaps the shrewd Wenlock thought it wise to pay more than the horse was really worth. Shortly before the old King died, Wenlock ordered that 40s. should be paid out of his funds, so that he could buy a new carriage for Prince Edward. Wenlock has even been accused of bribery when he presented gifts to King Edward II.

Immediately after his father's funeral, the Abbot gave the new King two pieces of silver plate and a sum of £40. He was criticized too, for giving a gilt cup and cover to Sir John de Charlton, a courtier attached to Gaveston. On one occasion Brother William de Chalk was sent to Northampton – the journey cost £2 – to present some silver gilt cups, which were worth £10. 12s. to Gaveston in person. Many suspected that these presents were really bribes to win the goodwill of the influential favourite.

Isabella of France gave birth to two sons, the future Edward III born at Windsor in November 1312, and John of Eltham born four years later and named thus because his birth occurred at the Royal Palace of Eltham in Kent. He was to play quite an important part during the early reign of his elder brother, for he acted on three occasions as regent of the kingdom during Edward III's absence abroad. John of Eltham was to die early in 1336, and his alabaster effigy in the Chapel of St Edmund in Westminster Abbey is of striking interest. How sad it is that we cannot today see the beautiful canopy which was once there, broken down it is said by the crowd at the funeral in 1776 of the Duchess of Northumberland in the Chapel of St Nicholas and removed by Dean Zachary Pearce. The small crowned figures round the sides of the tomb represent John of Eltham's grandparents Edward I, his second Queen Margaret of France, and his father and mother Edward II and Isabella of France.

Aymer de Valence, Earl of Pembroke, whose beautiful medieval tomb graces Westminster Abbey, had some affection for his cousin Edward II, and for some time possessed his trust. Though he lacked brilliance, he was an important personality and was frequently employed in negotiations with France. He negotiated the terms of the contract for Edward's marriage to Isabella daughter of Philip IV of France. His knowledge of Scotland made him indispensable as an adviser on Scottish affairs. In 1317 he was sent on a mission to Pope John XXII at Avignon to seek his help against the Scots and to try to regain control for the King of the revenues of the Duchy of Gascony. He was too honourable a man to take part in the execution of the hated Gaveston, when his enemies the Earls of Warwick "the Black Hound of Ardenne", Hereford and Arundel managed to take him prisoner by unscrupulous means during 1312. Aymer de Valence married twice. His first wife was a French lady, Beatrice, daughter of Ralph de Clermont, Lord of Nesle in Piccardy. His second marriage was to Marie de Saint-Pol, daughter of Guy de Chatillon, Count of Saint-Pol, a lady who was not only an aristocrat but of great ability and character. Aymer fortunately did not live to see Edward's horrible death, for he died in 1324. His wife founded a chantry in Aymer's memory, which now forms part of the Chapel of St John, but she is better known for the foundation of Pembroke College in Cambridge in 1347. She survived Aymer by over fifty years.

Neither Richard de Kedyngton, who succeeded Walter de Wenlock, as Abbot of Westminster in 1308, or William de Curtlington, who held this office seven years later, were distinguished abbots. Kedyngton had an unsavoury reputation, and the general impression abides, according to Westlake, that he was not a suitable person to rule the house.

Edward II had no very close associations with Westminster Abbey. He was religious by temperament, however, and once when staying at the Abbey of Bury St Edmunds as Prince of Wales, asked to be served with a monk's portion such as the brothers take in refectory. He founded an important Dominican brothers priory next to his favourite manor at Langley, and was a benefactor of St Albans Abbey.

The King learnt to hate his wife Isabella, saying that if he had no other weapon he would like to crush her with his own teeth. She was certainly cruel and vindictive and her adulterous relationship with her paramour Mortimer, Earl of March, disgusted many of her contemporaries. It was with her connivance and Mortimer's that Edward was murdered in Berkeley Castle in Gloucestershire in 1327. After his death the monks of Westminster made an attempt to obtain his body. Two brothers, Robert de Beby and John de Tothale travelled to Northampton where the Parliament was in session, but they failed to achieve their object. The remains of the wretched Edward were interred in the Abby Church of St Peter at Gloucester — now the Cathedral, though some believed that the Gloucester tomb did not contain Edward's body. It was his son Edward, now Edward III, who was responsible for raising the magnificent monument and effigy to his father's memory. After her husband's death, Isabella was allowed to live in retirement by her son, and died in Norfolk in 1358. She was buried in the Franciscan church at Newgate in London. She has this to her credit, that she was the mother of Edward III, one of the most chivalrous and remarkable of the Plantagenet kings.

After the deposition of his father, it was necessary for the boy King, Edward of Windsor, scarcely aged fourteen, to be elected King. Archbishop Reynolds presided at an assembly in Westminster Abbey on 20th January 1327. Before agreeing to accept his election, Prince Edward asked that it should be confirmed by his father.

Edward III was of medium height, so he was not as tall as his grandfather Edward I. He wore a short beard and had the most fascinating and gallant manners. When fierce rages possessed him his blue eyes smouldered like an active volcano. His hair has been described as neither red nor yellow, but a fair mixture of silver and gold. Edward's coronation took place in Westminster Abbey on 1st February 1327. Isabella his mother was present, and she is said to have wept throughout the ceremony, whether to dissemble her real feelings who can say? Edward's sword of state and shield of state were then first carried before him and afterwards in France.

The young Edward married a Flemish bride, Philippa of Hainault, a daughter of Count William of Hainault, at York Minster in January 1328. She was to prove one of the finest of our medieval Queens, a woman of strong character, who had a special affection for Westminster Abbey.

Philippa's coronation took place on 4th November 1330 in Westminster Abbey, while Edward was at his Palace of Eltham. The King wrote to command "his faithful Bartholomew de Burghersh to appear with his Barons of the Cinque Ports to do their customary duties at the coronation of his dearest Queen Philippa, which takes place, if God be propitious, the Sunday next to the Feast of St Peter ..." Bishop Grandisson of Exeter, however, wrote to Edward to excuse him from attending the ceremony on account of the difficulty of travel on the bad roads. This letter is in the Exeter archives.

She was much beloved in England because of her beautiful

character, and Froissart, the contemporary chronicler and her compatriot, paid her a striking tribute: "Tall and upright was she," he wrote, "wise, gay, humble, pious, liberal and courteous, decked and adorned in her time with all noble virtues, beloved of God and of mankind and so long as she lived, the Kingdom of England had favour, prosperity, honour, and every sort of good fortune ..." When Froissart came over to England in 1361, presenting her with a book about the war with France and the Battle of Poitiers, Philippa became his patron and made him her clerk or secretary. She gave him the facilities for travelling about the country, so that he could collect material for his books.

Philippa gave birth to her first son on 5th June 1330, at the Palace of Woodstock. It was Edward, later to be famous as the Black Prince, though he was first given this name in Grafton's Chronicle (1569) during the reign of the first Elizabeth. To his contemporaries he was known as Edward of Woodstock or 'Le Prince d'Angleterre'. Philippa bore Edward a large family – seven sons and three daughters.

Whether or not Edward III was a great King is a controversial matter. He was extremely chivalrous, and resembled a later French King, Louis XIV in his love of *gloire* (glory). He lacked the statesmanship of his grandfather Edward I. There is much substance in Sir Charles Oman's opinion that Edward III was selfish, thriftless, reckless of his country's needs, and set on gratifying his personal ambition and love of warlike feats to the sacrifice of every other consideration.

Philippa certainly exercised a beneficial influence on her husband, particularly at the siege of Calais in 1347, when six of the leading burgesses appeared before Edward in their shirts and with halters round their necks. The King wanted them put to death, but the gentle, merciful Queen pleaded for their lives, and Edward granted her request.

During his lifetime Edward III was more associated with Windsor Castle than Westminster Abbey. He built St George's Hall, and founded the most noble Order of the Garter about 1348, a small order of knighthood in which his own close companions and those of the Black Prince were the first founder members. The tradition is that a lady who Edward deeply admired dropped her blue garter at an entertainment at Windsor

Castle. The gallant Edward with an appropriate gesture put it on his own leg saying: *"Honi soit qui mal y pense"* ("Shame to him who thinks evil of it").

Edward of Woodstock, or the Black Prince, was much more attached to Christ Church, Canterbury than to Westminster Abbey, and his resplendent tomb is at Canterbury. Two children of Edward III and Philippa, William of Windsor and Blanche de la Tour (so called because of her birth in the Tower), are buried in St Edmund's Chapel. After Edward's younger brother John of Eltham died in 1336, the King wrote to the Abbot of Westminster, Thomas of Henley, desiring him to have John's body transferred to a more fitting place, the Chapel of St Edward, the burial place for royalty. This in fact never took place. It was Thomas of Henley who made a modest start with the building of the cloister.

Two remarkable Abbots presided at Westminster Abbey during Edward III's long reign of fifty years. These were Simon of Langham, better known as Abbot Langham, and Nicholas Littlington. Abbot Langham was a great benefactor to Westminster Abbey, and a brilliant administrator, though disliked by some of the Westminster monks and criticized as an ambitious schemer. He first came into prominence after the desolation of the Black Death (1348) – commemorated by Dean Stanley in Westminster Abbey by a plaque in the cloisters, when Abbot Byrcheston, described as a selfish and indolent man, and twenty-six monks were its victims. During 1353 there were only thirty monks who survived – among them Simon of Langham, known thus because he came from a village of that name in Rutland. Langham was appointed Abbot in 1349, and ruled Westminster Abbey for almost eleven years. It is evident that Langham was devoted to the interests of Westminster Abbey, and it may have been jealousy on the part of the others such as John of Reading, a monk of Westminster, which made them asperse Langham's motives. John of Reading relates that Abbot Langham's real object in giving Cardinals Talirand and Nicholas such sumptuous entertainment when they visited England to seek peace between England and France (1357) was sordid greed – the desire for fatter benefices. What harm is there if an able man such as Langham is ambitious, and is human enough to aspire to promotion in the Church? He was dictatorial and difficult to get on with, the type of man who is more respected than beloved by his colleagues and inferiors. Starting as abbot with debts of £2,500, Langham by his sagacious administration was able to pay off the debts during his period as Abbot. He also bought a number of manors for the convent of Westminster, and completed the building of the eastern walk of the cloister. He later planned the rebuilding of the nave. It is almost certain that Langham possessed large private means. Dr Hook in his *Lives of the Archbishops of Canterbury* supposes that on becoming a monk he assigned his private means to trustees "reserving that power over it which he so munificently displayed". Naturally it was one of the rules of the Benedictine order that monks were not allowed to possess private property. In the course of his duties he frequently came into contact with Edward III, who was a shrewd judge of character and formed a high opinion of him. Towards the end of 1360 he was appointed Lord High Treasurer of England. He might hold some of the highest offices in the state, but his heart was constant where Westminster Abbey was concerned. Having in mind that Henry III had given as a present to the Westminster monks eight fine bucks from Windsor Forest, Langham did not find it hard to persuade Edward that it would be a worthy act on his part to donate ten bucks to Westminster Abbey. A dispensation was required before the monks could do justice to the King's venison. The more spiritually minded monks were better pleased with two further gifts which Langham obtained from the King. These were the skull of St Benedict and the clothes in which St Peter the Apostle wore when he officiated.

Langham was appointed Bishop of Ely, and he has the distinction of being the only Abbot of Westminster who rose to the rank of Cardinal and then Archbishop of Canterbury 1366-1368. It was in the Chapel of St Nicholas that he was confirmed in the Archiepiscopal See. Edward III was at first furious when Pope Urban V, who was staying at Montefiascone, created Langham a cardinal. However, friendly relations were soon restored.

Close harmony and a sincere friendship existed between Simon Langham and Nicholas Littlington, who succeeded him as Abbot

of Westminster. He took the greatest possible interest in the plans
to rebuild Westminster Abbey. It was entirely owing to the
Cardinal's magnificent bequest that Littlington was able to
rebuild the Abbot's house (the present Deanery), and also parts
of the northern and the whole of the southern and western
cloisters. Nicholas Littlington was also devoted to Westminster
Abbey. He enjoyed the friendship of Edward III and was his
guest at Windsor Castle on two occasions. There was a rumour
that Littlington was in reality Edward's illegitimate son; Edward
is known to have had a mistress both during Philippa's lifetime
and after her death. The story almost certainly lacks foundation,
particularly as they were almost of the same age. Littlington's
favourite manor was at Denham and it was here and at Neyte
that John of Gaunt, fourth son of Edward (he was born in Ghent)
stayed with Littlington on three occasions. It seems that
Littlington was a less stern character than Langham. He was, for
instance, very fond of hunting and falconry as is proved by
entries in his accounts showing purchases of bows, bowstrings
and arrowheads. When the Abbot lost a favourite hen-falcon, he
was very upset. It was eventually found by the King's falconer
who was rewarded with a gift of 3s. 4d.

It is evident that Langham was in touch with French architects
and artisans who worked on the improvements in the Abbey
during the later fourteenth century. Parts of Westminster, such as
Petty France, remind us that it was the district where French
merchants trading with wool-staplers chiefly lived.

Cardinal Langham died in Avignon in 1376, a year before the
old King Edward III, but his body was not brought back to
Westminster for twelve years. In his will he had expressed a
desire to be buried in his beloved Abbey. In *A House of Kings —
The Official History of Westminster Abbey*, edited by the present
Dean, Edward Carpenter, we are told that Cardinal Langham
bequeathed to Westminster Abbey £7,800 (in cash, vestments
and books). Langham's monument is by Henry Yevele – greatest
of medieval architects. Yevele was assisted by the mason Stephen
Lote who came from Kent. The architect and the mason received
an instalment of £20 for the Langham tomb during the spring of
1395 when Edward's grandson Richard reigned as King.

Edward III's Parliament met regularly in the chapter house.

Through his endeavours, a national parliament, a national system of justice and a national army were created.

Few famous poets have been more closely associated with Westminster as Geoffrey Chaucer, born about 1340. His early important patron was John of Gaunt, and it was to commemorate the premature death of this prince's first wife, the enchanting Duchess Blanche of Lancaster in 1369, that Chaucer wrote an early poem "Dethe of Blaunche the Duchess". In his early life he was familiar with Edward III's court, serving as a yeoman of the King's chamber and later as a squire in the King's household. Those who wander around Westminster Hall may well be treading on the spot where the author of *The Canterbury Tales* lay down to sleep, bedded with a fellow yeoman as was the custom. Perhaps it was one of Chaucer's duties to taste the King's food for fear of poison or to carve for him.

Froissart's description of the last hours of Philippa of Hainault at Windsor Castle, who died eight years before her husband, is very sensitive and moving. She had been very kind to him. "When the good lady perceived her end approaching she called to the King, and extending her right hand from under the bed clothes, put it into the right hand of the King, who was very sorrowful at heart, and thus spoke, 'We have enjoyed our union in happiness, peace and prosperity. I entreat therefore of you, that on our separation you will grant me three requests.' The King with sighs and tears replied, 'Lady, ask. Whatever you request shall be granted.' After making various requests the Queen said, 'Thirdly I entreat that, when it shall please God to call you hence, you will not choose any other sepulchre than mine, and that you will lie by my side in the Cloisters of Westminster'. The King in tears replied, 'Lady, I grant them.' Thomas of Woodstock, who was later to oppose Edward's grandson Richard II, was her only son present on this lugubrious occasion. One suspects that Philippa on her death-bed was well aware of her Edward's infatuation for his mistress Alice Perrers, one of the women of her bedchamber.

England prospered so long as Philippa lived, but the last eight years of Edward's reign were calamitous for the country. Edward, too, in his inglorious decline is hardly an edifying subject. An elderly man, whether he be king or commoner, who is dominated by a rapacious mistress can only be an object of derision, or perhaps pity. Philippa's tomb in the St Edward Chapel is of black and white marble, and is of Flemish design. It is by a celebrated Flemish sculptor Hennequin de Liège, who worked in Paris. The King spent the large sum of £3,000 upon its erection. John Orchard, a bronze-worker of London was responsible for many of the images.

Edward III died at the ancient Palace of Sheen on 21st June 1377, deserted by his mistress, who, it is said, snatched the very rings from his fingers as he lay unconscious, and by the fickel courtiers.

Edward III's fine tomb was designed by Henry Yevele, who was at this period about fifty-five. The tomb is of Purbeck marble, and the gilt-bronze effigy in Westminster Abbey is probably by John Orchard. It seems a faithful likeness. With his flowing beard and finely chiselled face he is far removed from the cares of this world. Round the tomb now remain the carved figures of some of Edward's children, the Black Prince, Joan de la Tour, Lionel, Duke of Clarence, (an unlucky title), Edmund of Langley, Duke of York, Mary, Duchess of Britanny and William of Hatfield.

BIBLIOGRAPHY

Cammridge, John, *The Black Prince. An Historical Pageant* (1943)

Coulton, G.G., *Chaucer and his England* (3rd edition, 1921)

Edward I's Wardrobe Book 1296-97. MS. British Museum

Sir John Froissart's Chronicles Translated from the original French at the command of King Henry VIII by John Bourchier Lord Berners. Tr. Lord Berners (1523-5) Introduction by W.P. Ker 6 vols (1901-1903)

Geddes, Jane, "A Master Smith of the Middle Ages Thomas Leighton" (*Country Life* 14th August 1975)

Grafton's Chronicle (1569) (London 1809)

Hardy, B.C., *Philippa of Hainault and her Times* (1910)

Harvey, John, *Henry Yevele* (1944)

Hook, Walter Farquahar, *Lives of the Archbishops of Canterbury* Vols. IV, V, VI, IX (1860-1884)

Hutchinson, Harold F., *Edward II The Pliant King*
Oman, Sir Charles, *A History of England* (1921)
Pearce, E.H., *The Monks of Westminster* (1916) *Walter de Wenlock, Abbot of Westminster* (1920)
Phillips, J.R.S., *Aymer de Valence Earl of Pembroke* (1972)
Strickland, Agnes, *Lives of the Queens of England* Vol. I
Stubbs, Dr W., *The Early Plantagenets* (1876)

4

Richard II and Westminster Abbey

Richard II, who succeeded his grandfather on the throne in 1377, was a mere boy of ten. He was born in Bordeaux, the second son of Prince Edward of England, more familiarly known to us as 'the Black Prince'. His mother, Princess Joan was called the 'Fair Maid of Kent' because of her beauty. Sudbury the Archbishop of Canterbury described Richard in his youth as the very image of his father Edward, the Prince of Wales. There is a striking portrait of Richard just outside St George's Chapel in Westminster Abbey. The King is dressed in a crimson robe lined with ermine, and he wears a green vest. It is a picture of great beauty, and is almost certainly by a Frenchman, André Beauneveu of Valenciennes, portrait-painter to Charles V.

Richard was a tall man, six feet high. The contemporary chronicler Adam of Usk, an unfriendly critic in other respects, said that Richard was "fair among men even as another Absalom".

No king since Henry III has been more attached to Westminster Abbey than Richard. John Harvey in *The Plantagenets* described him as a highly intelligent and supremely cultured man. He was extremely religious, as is proved by his long hours at prayer at St Edward's Shrine before going out to meet the insurgents at Smithfield. Richard was a lover of the theatre, and devoted to the arts of the goldsmith, the jeweller and the embroiderer. He was the patron of an architect of genius, Henry Yevele, and a poet of genius Geoffrey Chaucer, appointed by King Richard as "Clerk of our works at our Palace of Westminster" and other offices.

Richard's coronation on 16th July 1377 has been described in great detail in the *Liber Regalis* by Abbot Littlington. It has indeed been the basis for all subsequent coronations, and the book is in the custody of the Deans of Westminster. For the first time we hear of a king of England in his cavalcade from the Tower, through Cheapside, Fleet Street and the Strand to Westminster. This custom continued until the time of Charles II, and his brother James later discontinued the practice. Now there is the first mention of the 'Knights of the Bath', favourite companions of Richard II, who escorted the King to his palace of Westminster. It was more than three centuries later that the actual Order of the Bath was instituted.

On the morning of his coronation, Richard rose early, wearing slippers or buskins only on his feet. William de Latymer's duty as almoner, assisted by deputies, was to cover the pavement from Westminster Hall to the regal seat, 'pulpitum' in the Abbey with red striped cloths. In the short procession to the Church of St Peter it was necessary for the King and others in the procession to traverse this carpet. The King's uncle, the celebrated John of Gaunt, "time-honoured Lancaster" as High Steward of England, bore the sword 'Curtana'. He was followed by Edmund, Earl of March carrying the second sword and spurs, which he bore on behalf of a minor, the Earl of Pembroke. Thomas of Woodstock, another uncle of the King, bore one royal baton and Edmund, Earl of Cambridge the other royal baton. Behind King Richard came Simon Sudbury, Archbishop of Canterbury, who was to crown him, and the Bishops of London and Winton. There was the sparkle, glitter and grandeur of a day of revelry, fountains gushing with wine, cloth of gold and the colourful costumes of the city guilds.

The bishops and nobles raised Richard up, and placed him in the Coronation Chair, so that he could be seen by those present. The Barons of the Cinque Ports held over the boy King a square awning or canopy of purple silk, supported on four silvered staves, ornamented with bells of silver gilt. No wonder that the elaborate, solemn service including the Mass, sermon, the presentation to and acceptance by the people, the enthronement and the crowning, was too much for Richard. Completely exhausted he had to be carried back to Westminster Palace on the shoulders of Sir Simon Burley, his tutor, who had been a favourite companion in arms of the Black Prince. The boy King impressed everybody with his regal dignity, although he lost a slipper whilst returning to the Palace.

On this occasion we first hear of the King's Champion, Sir John Dymoke, who was told by the Earl Marshal (as Dymoke had appeared too early on a magnificently caparisoned horse) to return when the King was at dinner in Westminster Hall. The last appearance of the King's Champion occurred at the magnificent coronation of George IV. John of Gaunt as Earl of Lincoln, had the right to carve before King Richard at the Coronation banquet.

The ritual made an enormous impression on the young King, giving him a lofty conception of the 'Divine Right of Kings'. Its beauty and all the colour must have appealed to his artistic nature. When Richard's first Parliament met at Westminster in October 1377, the despotic notions already forming in the King's mind, were encouraged by Sudbury's opening address when he referred to "the noble grace which God has given you, neither by election, nor by other such way, but only by right succession of heritage". He was not too young to understand the significance of Sudbury's speech.

Most people do not associate Westminster Abbey with scenes of violence, but murders and bloodshed have occurred there. During the fourteenth century and earlier, Westminster Abbey was one of the privileged, sacred places where people were allowed to take sanctuary in certain cases. It so happened that two former squires of the Black Prince, Robert Hawley and John Shakell, had captured the Spanish Count of Denia during the Najera campaign. They were entitled to considerable ransom money for their hostage. After the Count had been released on parole, his son was retained as hostage and security. The Count of Denia eventually negotiated for the ransom of his son, transmitting a portion of the money. The Council now eager to acquire the money, ordered the two squires to surrender their hostage. Hawley and Shakell refused and were consigned to the Tower. During August 1378 Hawley and Shakell, using violence, escaped from their far from irksome confinement, and took sanctuary in Westminster Abbey. Abbot Littlington was clearly within his rights to refuse to surrender the two men when a demand in the King's name was made. The Constable of the

Tower together with fifty soldiers broke into the Abbey sanctuary and captured Shakell, whom they took back to the Tower. Hawley, however, put up a stubborn resistance, and was murdered together with a sacrist named Richard, during High Mass in the Choir of St Peter's Church, a dreadful violation of the rights of sanctuary in this holy place. Bishop Courtenay of London took the courageous step of excommunicating those responsible for the crime, although he excluded young King Richard, his mother the Princess of Wales and John of Gaunt from the interdict, implying all the same that they were to some extent to blame.

As a result of this celebrated case, Westminster Abbey extended its right of sanctuary to debtors, mentioned by N.H. MacMichael Keeper of the Muniments in Westminster Abbey in an article in Occasional Papers 1970-73.

Another hideous example of the violation of sanctuary occurred during the Peasants' Revolt (1381) when Richard Imworth, Warder of the Marshalsea prison, fled for sanctuary to the Abbey. While Imworth clung to the pillars of the Shrine of St Edward the Confessor, the frenzied mob seized the wretched man, and hounded him to execution in Cheapside.

Richard II's first marriage to the gentle and devoted Anne of Bohemia, sister of King Wencelas of Bohemia, was idyllic. They deeply loved one another. The marriage was negotiated by Sir Simon Burley, and it took place in the Chapel of Westminster Palace in January 1382. Many resented the marriage because Anne brought no dowry. Goodness and a merciful disposition are more important qualities for a queen than mere physical beauty. It was William Courtenay who officiated at Anne's coronation as Archbishop of York. The pious Sudbury – a saintly man – had been barbarously and inexpertly executed by the ferocious rabble some time before. His head was stuck upon London Bridge where it remained for six days.

The King's veneration for Edward the Confessor was enormous, and his favourite oath was "By St Edward". The records show that he frequently attended Mass at St Edward's Altar before undertaking journeys. Richard's unconventional decision that several of his most intimate friends, people who had given him devoted service, but were not of royal blood, should be buried in St Edward's Chapel among the Kings, was keenly resented by the nobility. John of Waltham, Bishop of Salisbury, who held various high offices of state, was by Richard's order buried next to Edward I in St Edward's Chapel. It is unlikely that the Abbey authorities shared in the indignation of some of the barons, for the King gave them costly presents of two splendid copes and a large sum of money.

Another great favourite of the King, Sir John Golofre, second husband of Philippa, Duchess of York, who had been Richard's ambassador in France, was first buried close to his master's tomb. Today he lies in the St Edmund Chapel. Nearby is Sir Bernard Brocas, who held high office at Richard's Court, father of the knight of the same name who was executed on Tower Hill for having joined in a conspiracy with the object of reinstating Richard on the throne in 1400. Father and son were famous for their Spanish connection with Brozas near Alcántara, and one of these doughty warriors had fought with the Moors.

Sir John Froissart mentions the cruel manner of the younger Sir Bernard's death, "along with four knights tyed to two horses in the presence of them that were in the Towre, and the Kynge myght well se it out of the wyndowes wherewith he was sore discomforted ..."

With the possible exception of Langham, no medieval abbot did more for the Abbey of Westminster than Littlington. Not only did he build a large addition to the nave, but he was responsible for part of the abbot's house, including the Jerusalem Chamber. One striking achievement was the paintings which he ordered to be placed around the cloister walls, in the abbot's hall, and on the nave walls. According to *The House of Kings*, it was probably Littlington who glazed the cloister arcades with stained glass. He was certainly a patriot, for on hearing of a threatened invasion of our shores by the King of France in 1386, Abbot Littlington with two of his monks John Canterbury and John Burgh, wished to don full armour and go as far as the coast. It was only the infirmities of old age which prevented the man from carrying out this resolve. The Abbot died at the end of November and was succeeded by William of Colchester, who was Shakespeare's Abbot of Westminster in *Richard II*. It is curious however that William of Colchester's appointment was at first opposed by King Richard, since Colchester later supported the King and conspired on his behalf before his deposition. Richard favoured the candidature of Brother John la Kyngheth the treasurer. Colchester was, however, installed as Abbot on 12th October 1387, and on the following day, St Edward's Day, entertained his friends to a sumptuous banquet. A study of the Calendar of Close Rolls* makes it clear that Pope Urban confirmed the election. When Richard II walked barefoot from Charing to the entrance of the Abbey, it was Abbot Colchester and his monks in their vestments, who received him. It was his predecessor Littlington, who had been impressed with Colchester's administrative gifts and selected him as 'Custos Hospicii', or Seneschal Steward of his household. Littlington used Colchester in managing his many business interests, for he held various rent-rolls in parts of England, including Gloucester, Worcester, Surrey, Oxford and Middlesex. One of the more humble of his duties was to arrange for Abbot Littlington's boots to be repaired for twopence. When the Squire of the Earl of Cambridge, Edmund of Langley (later Duke of York), a younger son of Edward III, brought a letter from his master to the Abbot, it was Colchester who saw to it that the messenger received 20s. as a reward. Owing to his ability, William of Colchester was chosen as Convent Treasurer and 'Coquinarius' or Kitchener, for the year 1375-1376. Here is one of the items entered by Colchester: "Paid in milk, 'creym', butter, cheese and eggs bought for the pancakes in Easter week, on Rogation days and at Pentecost, 68s. 4d." During the following years Colchester was employed on confidential missions abroad.

Richard was unfortunate in his enemies, the caucus of appellant Lords, who secured the condemnation of some of his friends in 1388, among them Sir Simon Burley. Anne of Bohemia kneeling at the feet of the ruthless Thomas of Woodstock now Duke of Gloucester, pleaded in vain for Sir Simon's life, but he was executed. Froissart wrote emotionally: "God have mercy on his soule. To write of his shameful dethe ryght sore displeaseth me ... The Queen also was sorie and wepte for his dethe bycause he

* Enrolments kept in Chancery of various documents sent out to offices throughout the country and overseas.

fetched her out of Almaygne (Germany)". Another of Richard's most intimate friends Robert de Vere, Earl of Oxford died in exile.

It was in 1394 that Richard's beloved Queen Anne of Bohemia died at the Palace of Sheen where they had known happiness together. So violent was Richard's grief that he ordered Sheen to be razed to the ground. The Queen was given a magnificent funeral, her body first lying in state at St Paul's, then carried in procession to the burial service in Westminster Abbey. It is recorded that an abundance of wax was sent from Flanders for flambeaux and torches, so that the illumination was exceedingly bright. Thomas Arundel, a future Archbishop of Canterbury, (Earl Richard's brother) preached the funeral sermon and praised the Queen's character. One ugly incident marred the ceremony. With gross ill manners, Richard Fitzalan, Earl of Arundel, ostentatiously absented himself from St Paul's and arrived late in Westminster Abbey. Richard was so incensed when Arundel asked to be excused before the service was over that he seized a wand from one of the vergers and struck the Earl so violently that he fell to the ground, his blood spilling on the Abbey pavement. Richard may be criticized for his complete lack of control in the sacred precincts of the Abbey, but Arundel was also to blame. Richard erected a magnificent tomb for his Queen. Anne's gilt-bronze effigy in Westminster Abbey was by Nicholas Broker and Godfrey Prest.

Anne had a moderating influence on Richard, and his character deteriorated after her death. Though their marriage had been so blessed, it had not been enriched by offspring, as the Kirkstall Abbey Chronicles relate.

Richard's second marriage to Isabelle of France, daughter of Charles VI, was a political marriage. The Princess was only eight years old. She made her state entry into London in the autumn of 1396, and on 7th January she was crowned Queen in Westminster Abbey. Richard grew fond of his child bride.

King Richard had been charged with the murdering of his uncle, Gloucester (Thomas of Woodstock) by having him smothered under a feather bed in Calais, but the matter is open to doubt. Certainly Richard had reasons for hating Gloucester because of his uncle's diabolical plotting against him. At Council meetings he was both boorish and domineering. Thomas of Woodstock was first buried in St Edmund's Chapel in Westminster Abbey, but his body was later removed to the St Edward Chapel. After his death his widow Eleanor de Bohun a great heiress, became a nun at Barking. She died in 1399 and was buried in the St Edmund Chapel. Her tomb contains the finest brass in the Abbey.

Adam of Usk tells of the celebrated quarrel between Thomas Mowbray, Duke of Norfolk, and Henry Bolingbroke, Duke of Hereford, when Bolingbroke accused Norfolk of high treason. Between Richard and his cousin Bolingbroke — he was John of Gaunt's son — there always existed a latent jealousy, for they were entirely dissimilar in temperament. When Earl of Derby, Bolingbroke, an opportunist, had treacherously plotted against the King. The King sentenced his cousin Hereford to ten years banishment from the realm, while Norfolk was given the harsher punishment of perpetual exile. As Richard's friend the loyal Bishop of Carlisle tells us in Shakespeare's *Richard II*, Norfolk eventually

"toil'd with works of war, retir'd himself to Italy, and there at Venice gave his body to that pleasant country's earth".

In February 1399 there died old John of Gaunt, "time-honoured Lancaster". Adam of Usk relates that Richard's uncle was buried near the altar in St Paul's Church (Cathedral). Richard's greatest political mistake with the support of the Council was to confiscate Henry Bolingbroke's enormous Lancastrian estates. While Richard was absent from the kingdom engaged in his second Irish expedition, Bolingbroke landed at Ravenspur at the northern point of the Humber estuary. Within three weeks Bolingbroke had most of England behind him. At Pontefract he published the falsehood that Edmund Crouchback, younger son of Henry III, from whom he was descended, was the elder brother of Edward I, and had been set aside because of his deformities. At the same time, Henry Bolingbroke swore a solemn oath to Henry Percy, Earl of Northumberland that he had only come to England to claim his rightful inheritance, an oath which the perjured Henry, on becoming Henry IV, soon broke.

On 30th September 1399, a large but unruly assembly of representatives of the estates of Parliament and London citizens, met in Westminster Great Hall. It was in this historic setting that the instrument of abdication was signed by Richard. Thirty-three articles of accusation—the so-called "gravamina" were read aloud, whereupon the "estates of the Realm" decided that the King should be deposed. It was here that Hugh Herland, who sprang from a family connected for two generations with the King's carpentry works, had built his masterpiece the hammer-beam roof between 1394-1400. Among those who protested at the proceedings was the brave Thomas Merks or Merke, Bishop of Carlisle. Richard had been his patron and friend. He had been a monk of Westminster, and was a close friend of William of Colchester, Abbot of Westminster. He once wrote to Colchester, "For they see your steadfastness (*solidatem*), which is a rare virtue in these modern days, and because of it, look to you especially." In his portrayal of the character of the Bishop of Carlisle, Shakespeare keeps closer to historical truth than in his brief references to the Abbot of Westminster (William of Colchester), who evidently was involved in a conspiracy to reinstate Richard on the throne. Here Shakespeare takes dramatic licence. However, the dramatist had no doubt read the Chronicler Hall's account of what happened in Westminster Hall when Carlisle claimed that there was nobody competent and fit to judge such a sovereign as Richard II "whom we have acknowledged our Lord for the space of twenty years or more". Shakespeare puts into the mouth of Carlisle these words:

Would God that any in this noble presence
were enough noble to be upright judge
of noble Richard.

He then goes on to condemn Henry Bolingbroke as a foul traitor.

Carlisle was accused of treason and languished for a time in chains in the Tower of London. After being released, he was sent to the Abbey of Westminster where he led the life of a monk. He was brought to trial, found guilty and deprived of his bishopric. From the Tower he was handed over to the custody of

the Abbot of Westminster. He was later pardoned. In all fairness
to Henry IV Carlisle was treated with leniency and generosity.
He respected his valiant enemy,

For though mine enemy thou hast ever been,
High sparks of honour in thee have I seen.

Carlisle lived quietly in retirement and died rector of Todenham
in Gloucestershire in 1409.

William of Colchester's part in a conspiracy to reinstate the
fallen Richard to the throne is rather obscure. The Abbot of
Westminster plotted with the Bishop of Carlisle and others to
storm Windsor Castle and capture Henry and his son dead or
alive. Unfortunately the conspiracy was betrayed to the new
King Henry by one of those involved in it. It was at supper in the
Abbot's lodgings that he, Carlisle and others planned their plots.
One thing is certain "that the grand conspirator, Abbot of
Westminster, with clog of conscience and some melancholy" did
not die at this juncture (as Shakespeare alleges). Colchester
remained Abbot of Westminster, though committed to the
Tower during 1400 after the accession of Henry IV. We find him
during the reign of Henry V among a delegation of envoys
including the Prior of Worcester and the Earl of Warwick, sent
to attend the Council of Constance in 1414. It was during
Richard's reign that Colchester superintended the rebuilding of
the nave in Westminster Abbey, and Richard supplied various
gifts of money. William of Colchester died in 1420, and his tomb
is in St John the Baptist's Chapel. If only he could return to life,
what stories could he tell of secret plots in the Abbot's house
when the conspirators dined and wined together?

Richard was so closely associated in the popular mind with
Westminster Abbey, that during this time of adversity, the
citizens of London, thinking he had fled there, armed themselves
and searched in vain for the King in the Abbey. They found,
however, three Counsellors, Roger Walden, Nicholas Slake and
Ralph Selby, whom they ordered to be kept in custody. Nicholas
Slake was prebendary of York, and a dean of the King's Chapel,
Westminster.

Richard's death in Pontefract Castle in York was certainly

mysterious. There is probably no truth in the story that Sir Pierce of Exton murdered Richard, as related by Shakespeare. Adam of Usk relates that the late King "as he lay in chains in the Castle of Pontefract, was tormented by Sir Thomas Swinford with starving fare". This is the only contemporary chronicle which accused an individual of starving their illustrious prisoner. It may well be that Richard voluntarily abstained from food as Walsingham alleges. The Kirkstall Chronicle states: "God alone knows the truth of the manner of his death, a little after the feast of the purification of the glorious virgin." His body was taken to Cheapside and St Paul's, where 20,000 people saw Richard exposed to view. He was buried without ceremony in the Dominican priory of King's Langley in Hertfordshire. It was only on 4th December 1413 that Henry V, who revered the memory of Richard II, had his body brought with great honour to Westminster Abbey. There he lies as is fitting enough by the side of his first wife Anne of Bohemia, who he loved so deeply. Adam of Usk commented: "My God! How many thousand marks he spent on burial places of vain glory for himself and his wives." (Isabelle, his child-wife, was not buried in the Abbey among the kings at Westminster).

Henry IV was crowned in Westminster Abbey on St Edward's Day, 13th October 1399. He spent so long with his confessor that morning, possibly tormented by his conscience, that he arrived late at the Abbey. It was noticed while the King was being anointed that there was a great growth of lice, especially on his head. Holinshed gives the names of the forty-six new Knights of the Bath created by Henry IV. There was considerable splendour, for all the peers of the realm wore red, scarlet and ermine. Henry Percy, Earl of Northumberland, who was soon to rebel against his master, carried the first sword, and the sword of justice was born by the new King's eldest son the Prince of Wales. The Lord Latimer bore the sceptre and the Earl of Westmorland the rod. During the coronation banquet which followed, the Earl of Arundel was butler, and Sir Thomas Erpingham one of Henry's stoutest supporters served the office of chamberlain.

Once again the King's champion Sir Thomas Dymoke appeared at the coronation feast, entering Westminster Hall mounted in full armour on a charger, and having his sword sheathed in black with a golden hilt. On his instructions a herald proclaimed at the four sides of the hall that if any man should say that his liège lord here present and King of England was not of right King of England, he was ready to prove the contrary with his body. Some of those present must have been apprehensive lest somebody might take up the challenge, whereupon Henry IV said: "If need be, Sir Thomas, I will in mine own person ease thee of this office." Henry's Queen Joanna of Navarre was crowned on 26th February 1403, in Westminster Abbey.

It can hardly be wondered at that Henry IV had little affection for Westminster Abbey, remembering as he did that its Abbot and many of the monks had favoured Richard. Unlike his predecessor, Henry did little for art, merely ordering Master William Colchester the Abbey's Chief Mason to travel to York in 1407 to take charge of the building of the central tower of York Minster, which had recently collapsed. The York masons were furious that William Colchester had been charged with this work, and gravely wounded him. The continuation of the work on the nave in Westminster Abbey was postponed.

Henry lacked his cousin Richard's arresting good looks. He was short and reddish haired, but he was certainly tough. As might be expected Henry, as the son of John of Gaunt, and Blanche of Lancaster (his first wife), was a man of culture. He was deeply interested in music as revealed by Frank Le Harrison in his *Music in Medieval Britain* (1958). John Streche, the Canon of Kenilworth, stated that Henry was himself a brilliant musician. He may have played the flute or recorder, and his first wife Mary de Bohun sang. Froissart described Henry's mother, Blanche, so greatly loved by her contemporaries, "gay and glad she was, fresh and sportive, sweet simple and of humble semblance, the fair lady whom men called Blanche". Yet Henry was not an endearing character. For the remainder of his life he was haunted by a consciousness of guilt. Others conspired against him such as Richard Scrope, Archbishop of York, even as Henry had conspired against Richard. After the death of this prelate Henry's health deteriorated, and contemporaries affirm that his features were disfigured by the disease of leprosy.

At least it can be said of Henry that he was generous to

Chaucer, who had been deprived of his office of Clerk of Works at the Palace of Westminster in 1391 by Richard II. After all Henry was son of the poet's most important patron, John of Gaunt. Chaucer had been granted a pension by Richard II of £20 per annum, and Henry IV allowed him a pension of 40 marks. For a period Chaucer leased from Westminster Abbey "a tenement with its appartenances situate in the garden of St Mary's Chapel", on the site of the present Henry VII's Chapel. Chaucer only enjoyed his affluence for a short time, for he died on 25th October 1400, and his monument in Poets' Corner is the Abbey's first literary monument.

It is well known that Henry IV died in the Jerusalem Chamber in Westminster Abbey when he was contemplating an expedition to the Holy Land in 1413. While the ailing King was praying before St Edward's Shrine he was taken desperately ill and had to be carried through the cloisters into the Abbot's Place. He was brought to the Jerusalem Chamber and laid on a pallet. The cheerful fire on that chilly spring day lightened his spirits. When he recovered from his swoon, he inquired of his attendants, whether the room where he lay had any special name. Shakespeare in immortal poetry has related what then occurred.

Warwick   'Tis call'd Jerusalem, my noble lord.
King Henry   Laud be to God! even there my life must end.
               It hath been prophesied to me many years
               I should not die but in Jerusalem,
               Which vainly I suppos'd the Holy Land.
               But bear me to that chamber, there I'll lie.
               In that Jerusalem shall Harry die.

Visitors to this historic and beautiful room, as they are taken round by a verger, may well ponder that it was here that the Prince of Wales, the future Henry V, tried on his father's crown. The story rests on tradition, and the scene has been dramatized by Shakespeare. In the ancient Palace of Westminster the King, reflecting on the treasonable activities of Henry Percy, Earl of Northumberland, and others, at last became aware that men reap what they sow in this life.

Such things become the hatch and brood of time;
And by the necessary form of this,
King Richard might create a perfect guess
That great Northumberland, then false to him,
Would of that seed grow to a greater falseness.
Which should not find a ground to root upon
Unless on you.*

In such a way the poet-philosopher makes the Earl of
Warwick address his King in Part II of *Henry IV*, one of the
finest of the historical plays. Henry, however, like his uncle the
Black Prince, was buried in Canterbury Cathedral where a
monument was raised to his memory. There he lies together with
Joanna of Navarre, the only sovereign to be interred in that
resplendent place.

BIBLIOGRAPHY

Adam of Usk (ed. Maunde Thompson), *Chronicon* (1377-1404) with
    translation London 1904. Second Edition. Very Lancastrian in
    outlook.
Armitage-Smith, Sydney, *John of Gaunt, King of Castile and Leon* (1904)
Harrison, Frank Le. *Music in Medieval Britain* (1958)
Hutchinson, Harold F., *The Hollow Crown* (1961)
Kirby, J.L., *Henry IV of England* (1970)
The Kirkstall Chronicle 1355-1400 (ed. M.V. Clarke and N.
    Denholme-Young) Manchester 1931
Chronicles of Froissart (Globe Edition). Macmillan 1913
Liber Regalis. Account of Richard II's coronation by Abbot Littlington.
    Printed for the Roxburghe Club (1880)
MacMichael, N.H., *Sanctuary at Westminster*. Occasional Papers 1970-
    73
Shakespeare, William, *Richard II*
Shakespeare, William, *Henry IV* Part I and II
Shakespeare, William, *Henry VIII*

* *Henry IV* Part 2 Act III Scene II

Tanner, Dr Laurence, *Recollections of a Westminster Antiquary*
Tanner, Dr Laurence, *The History and Treasures of Westminster Abbey* (1953)
Tanner, Dr Laurence, *The Abbot's House and the Deanery of Westminster Abbey*

5

Henry V and Westminster Abbey

We are so accustomed to regard Henry V as a great warrior-king, the hero of Agincourt, that we tend to forget that his character had many other aspects. He was deeply religious after his accession to the throne, even if he was naturally influenced by his age. His piety was narrow. Like Richard II he had a love and a veneration for Westminster Abbey and during his short reign he was a constant benefactor. Henry's supposed wildness, frivolity and fondness for the society of profligate and unworthy people during his youth rests on some solid foundation, but it is certain that after his father's death some spiritual experience made such a profound impression on his mind that he underwent a conversion. Thomas Elmham, a monk of Canterbury, wrote that when young, Henry was a diligent follower of idle practices.

The contemporary historian Thomas Walsingham, writing within six years of his accession, states that at Henry's coronation he was suddenly transformed into a new man in gravity, honesty and moderation. No King was more a child of his age. Henry was both priggish and fanatical. He regularly attended Mass and was liberal in alms-giving.

The chronicler Hall gives us a physical description of the King: "He was of stature more than the common sort, of body lean, well-membered and strongly made, a face beautiful, somewhat long-necked, black-haired (actually it was brown). His eyes were brown and glowed with light, dovelike when unmoved, but fierce as a lion when roused."

It is said that immediately after his father's death, Henry went in secret to the cell of a recluse in the precincts of Westminster Abbey, probably William Alnwick, and spent several hours in confession and prayer with him. Laurence Tanner, former keeper of the muniments has revealed in his work *History and Treasures of Westminster Abbey*, that the probable door of this cell is now in Poets' Corner.

Henry's coronation is chiefly memorable because of a terrible blizzard, and several feet of deep snow lay thick in Westminster. On 7th April 1413 Henry had ridden through London to the Tower where he had knighted some fifty candidates who had passed the night in vigil over their arms in the Norman chapel of St John. The new knights, with a great rout of lords, escorted the King in state through the Cheap to the Palace of Westminster. Henry was crowned on Passion Sunday, 9th April 1413 in the Abbey Church by Thomas Arundel, Archbishop of Canterbury. For the occasion a stage or scaffold draped with cloth of gold had been erected between the high altar and the choir. Henry's coronation is the only one to be represented in sculpture on each side of his chantry.

It was noticed at the coronation banquet that Henry looked unusually pensive and serious and that he ate almost nothing. Other favoured guests no doubt did justice to the flampets of fat pork and figs boiled in small ale with cheese, fried in clean grease and then baked in a coffin of paste and coloured with the yolk of eggs. Henry V's biographer, James Hamilton Wylie, mentions that the royal cooks had made sugar, paste or jelly into antelopes, gilded eagles or swans and cygnets. These curious devices sat on green stocks with scriptures or subscriptions in pastry coming out of their mouths calling upon the King "to keep the law and guard the foi" and "have pitee on the commonaltee". Servants on horseback brought in the steaming dishes. They must have acquired much skill in striking a balance.

Henry spent Easter in 1413 at Langley. Here, we are told, he gave 4d. apiece to 3000 poor people at the Royal Maundy, a very ancient ceremony. It was in December that King Henry ordered that King Richard II's body should be brought to Westminster, to be buried in his own tomb in the Abbey. A host of bishops, abbots, lords and knights escorted the procession. People scrambled for the largesse of 1000 marks, which were distributed on the route. The King attended the service and ordered that four large tapers were to burn continually at Richard's tomb.

Richard II had been much attached to Henry in his boyhood,

and had given him an income of £500 per annum. He told him that he believed he was destined to fulfil the prophecy of Merlin that a prince should be born in Wales (Henry was born at Monmouth), whose fame and praise would one day resound throughout the world. It was therefore now fitting for Henry to make reparation to Richard's memory, and he may too have possessed a warm regard for the former King.

Henry V inherited his father's love of music, and he could play the harp. It was an interest which he shared with his French wife, Katharine de Valois. Agnes Strickland relates that by the hands of William Menston was paid £8. 13s. 4d. for two new harps purchased for the royal couple. When in France the King had another harp sent to him by John Bore, the best harp-maker in London. Henry was a patron of three of the most important composers of the fifteenth century, Thomas Damet, Nicholas Sturgeon and John Pyamour. A Song School was founded by Henry at Durham, and he delighted in church harmony.

Henry's Queen Katharine, daughter of Charles VI of France, was crowned in Westminster Abbey by Archbishop Chicheley of Canterbury on 24th February 1421. This ceremony was attended by James I of Scotland, who sat next to Katharine at the coronation feast. Since it was Lent, fish-dishes were mainly served, including dead eels, stewed. For the second course there were all sorts of delicacies including crayfish or lobsters, and fresh baked lampreys.

It is, perhaps, little known that Henry endowed monasteries at Sheen in Surrey and near Brentford, but his work in the rebuilding of the nave of Westminster Abbey was much more important. The King acted with his customary energy. On learning that the nave was "long in ruins and undone", Henry immediately contributed 100 marks for the new work, and commanded the mayor of London to employ carpenters, workmen and stone-cutters for the operations. During December 1413 the King raised his contribution to 1000 marks per annum for completing the nave. This money was partly raised from fees in chancery, and partly obtained from charges on the customs of the Port of London. The King's cousin Edward, Duke of York, and Bishop Henry Beaufort supervised the work. The administrative and financial arrangements were in the hands of

Richard Whityington, Collector of the Customs and Richard Harweden, a monk at Westminster, who later became Abbot. Richard Whityngton (died 1423) was indeed a celebrated mayor of London on several occasions, and there is the story of the cat who brought him good fortune. It is certainly true that Henry V borrowed from Whityington, and to some extent gave him his trust. As a benefactor, Whityington has been described as the last of the great medieval mayors of London. A beautiful stained glass window in the north transept commemorates both King Henry and Whityington, nor is the cat forgotten. Actually it was William Colchester, master-mason in the Abbey, who supervised the carpenters. He was simultaneously employed on the operations at York Minster. His fee in the Abbey was £10 per annum. The administrative problem of paying the men, providing the tools of their trade and giving them food, was by no means a light one. It required much organization for the stone to be quarried at Bere in Dorset and Reigate in Surrey, and Stapleton in Yorkshire, and to be transported to Westminster. Caen stone from Normandy was used for the finer parts.

Among the medieval Kings, Henry deserves more tributes than he has been given for the rebuilding of the nave, and he altogether contributed £3,861. At his death the walls to the extent of six bays had been completed through the triforium and as far as the clerestory.

Like most of the Plantagenets, Henry loved hunting, and when away on one of his expeditions, he would present the monks of Westminster with game, even as Henry III was wont to do in the thirteenth century. He restored to them a ruby ring valued at 1000 marks, which had been given to the Shrine of Edward the Confessor by Richard II.

In his religious opinions, Henry was orthodox, bigoted, and anxious to stamp out heresy. Considering the fifteenth century, the age in which he lived, he cannot be charged with cruelty, although he was once present at the burning of a Lollard named John Badby, a tailor. The Lollards wanted an older and purer form of religion, deriving their inspiration from reading the new English bible. They believed that confession was not necessary for salvation, but their main teachings were strongly anti-papist and opposed to the priests.

The left-hand panel of the Wilton Diptych, depicting Richard II
kneeling in prayer to the Virgin. Behind him are three patron saints:
Edward the Martyr, Edward the Confessor holding his ring, and
St John the Baptist

Henry V's Chantry Chapel

Shakespeare has immortalized Henry's famous victory at Agincourt, fought on St Crispin's Day, 25th October 1415, and a Te Deum service of thanksgiving was held before St Edward's Shrine. In Henry's Chantry Chapel in Westminster Abbey there is the sculptured figure of Henry V at Agincourt in full armour on his horse.

Henry V died at his favourite Castle of Vincennes on 31st August 1422. His funeral was one of the most magnificent ever to take place in Westminster Abbey. The slow and stately procession bore the King's body to St Denis, burial-place of the kings of France and then to Rouen through Abbeville, Boulogne to Calais. Four powerful black horses drew the coffin, and the chief mourners were the widowed Queen Katharine and King James I of Scotland. His body first lay in state in St Paul's Cathedral, and was then borne to the Abbey on 7th November. His effigy was carried on the funeral car, escorted by numerous white-robed priests chanting their prayers. Many citizens of London took part and from the Church of St Magnus to Temple Bar a torch-bearer stood before every house. During the Abbey service, Henry's three chargers were lead up to the altar. Henry's tomb was made of the finest materials, Caen stone and Purbeck marble. In his will, Henry had directed that a high chantry chapel should be raised over his body. This was the work of John of Thirske, the architect of the nave at this period. Throughout the centuries Henry has remained a strong attraction to visitors desiring to see the St Edward Chapel. They are eager to see his shield and saddle, and his tilting helmet which tradition says was worn by the King at Agincourt. Among the Plantagenets, Henry ranks high but he was not so great as Edward I.

It is a melancholy reflection that men of powerful personality such as Edward I and Henry V, should have weaklings as their sons. Henry VI, who succeeded to the throne aged only nine, was totally unfitted by temperament to rule over the turbulent England of the fifteenth century. As founder of Eton College he would have made a good monk. Yet one can imagine the little boy at his coronation on 6th November 1429, seated on the platform in the Abbey, gazing about him, slightly puzzled at all the pomp and splendour, "beholding all the people about sadly and wisely". So he was crowned by Archbishop Chicheley.

Henry married Margaret of Anjou in Titchfield Abbey, a woman of dominating character whose father René was the second son of Louis II, King of Sicily and Jerusalem, and Count of Provence. She was crowned in Westminster Abbey in 1445. To celebrate her coronation, brilliant tournaments were held at Westminster, which lasted three days. Henry and Margaret had one son, Edward, born on St Edward's Day, but Holinshed mentions that the common people had "such an opinion of the King that they sticked not to saie, that this was not his sonne, with many slanderous words greatly sounding to the Queen's dishonour". Certainly the young prince resembled his mother in character rather than his father.

None of the Abbots of Westminster during the troubled reign of Henry, were outstanding. William of Colchester had died in 1420, and Richard Harweden resigned the abbacy twenty years later, probably because of debts and misgovernment. Abbot Edmund Kirton, his successor, had an evil reputation for immorality, but managed to retain his office until 1463, when Edward IV was on the throne.

Henry VI was attached to Westminster Abbey, and was in the habit of paying many visits to St Edward's Chapel, escorted by Abbot Kyrton, who received him by torchlight at the postern. Henry certainly planned a tomb for himself in the Lady Chapel. Once when visiting his father's Chantry Chapel, it was suggested to Henry that the tomb of Henry V might be moved a little to make way for his own tomb. The King replied: "Nay, let him alone; he lieth like a noble prince. I wolle not trouble him." Henry pondered deeply, and then remarked: "Forsooth, forsooth, here will we lie. Here is a good place for us." The Abbey Mason, John of Thirske took an iron instrument and marked the place where Henry wanted to be buried. The tomb was actually ordered but the pathetic Henry, who was murdered in the Tower of London in 1471, was eventually buried in St George's Chapel, Windsor, his birth-place.

Henry's mother, Queen Katharine, is however buried in the Abbey. The widowed Queen had soon succumbed to the charms of a handsome Welshman named Owen Tudor after her husband's death. He came of ancient lineage, and is said to have fought with gallantry at Agincourt. He became one of the esquires of the body to Henry V and later clerk of the wardrobe to Katharine. It was noticed by the Queen's ladies that Katharine was much attracted to Owen, especially when he fell into her lap after making too elaborate a pirouette whilst dancing. They were secretly married, but the Council, furious on discovering what had happened, persecuted both Queen Katharine and her Welsh lover. She was confined in Bermondsey Abbey, while Owen Tudor for a time took sanctuary at Westminster where he was wont to brag of his adventures at Agincourt. By Owen, Katharine had three sons, Edmund, created Earl of Richmond who was married to Lady Margaret Beaufort. They were parents of the future Henry VII. Jasper became Earl of Pembroke, while Edward Tudor was more intimately associated with the Abbey than his brothers, for he lived and died a monk of Westminster. He lies today in Poets' Corner, and each time I pass his tablet I think of this strange man, the uncle of Henry VII our first Tudor king. Camden records his burial in the Chapel of St Blaise.

Katharine died on 3rd January 1437, at Bermondsey. Her body was first removed to the church of her patroness, St Katharine by the Tower, and later brought to Westminster Abbey where she was buried in Henry III's Lady Chapel. Her son Henry VI and his Queen attended the funeral in state. It was Henry VII who built the chapel always associated with his name. In erecting it, it was necessary to demolish the old Lady Chapel, and Henry later arranged for his grandmother's body to be buried by the side of her husband in Henry V's Chantry Chapel. To reach it one ascends a narrow turret staircase, and since it is not usually open to our many visitors I had been given permission by the late Dean's Verger, Mr Greaves to see it. How beautiful it is in the austere light to look down on the Confessor's Chapel. Many years after Katharine's death on 23rd February 1668-69, Samuel Pepys saw "by particular favour" her body. In his snobbish way he insisted on kissing her mouth, and delighted that he had kissed a Queen on his thirty-sixth birthday.

Henry V, who had greatly admired Richard II, saw to it that his favourite clerics, such as Richard Courtenay, Bishop of Norwich, should be buried in the St Edward's Chapel. This is reminiscent of Richard, who was criticized for his fondness for burying his favourites in the Confessor's Chapel, and in St Edmund's Chapel. Courtenay is now buried in the north turret of Henry V's Chantry Chapel. Sir Lewis Robessart, the King's standard-bearer at Agincourt, was interred in St Paul's Chapel in 1431.

The internecine Wars of the Roses between the Houses of Lancaster and York dominated events during the later fifteenth century. After Edward IV succeeded in gaining the throne from Henry in 1461, he was crowned in Westminster Abbey on 29th June by Archbishop Bourchier. Edward was tall and handsome, popularly known as the 'White Rose of Rouen' because he had been born in Rouen. He was pleasure-loving and sensual, fond of seducing the wives of city magnates. Underneath his air of apparent indolence he hid much ability.

From the Tower, Edward made his way to Westminster Abbey, followed by thirty-two Knights of the Bath he had created as a reward for their valiant service. They were hooded in silk like priests, and wore pieces of white silk over their left shoulders. Dressed in his royal robes, but not wearing the crown, Edward was anointed by the Archbishops of Canterbury and York before the high altar. Then holding the sceptre and wearing the Cap of Estate, St Edward's Crown was placed on his head. For the coronation banquet delicacies such as peacocks, pheasants and swans were prepared.

Edward secretly married Elizabeth Woodville, the beautiful widow of a Lancastrian knight Sir John Grey, at Grafton Regis in Northamptonshire on May Day 1464, much to the consternation of the king-maker Richard Neville, Earl of Warwick and others when they later discovered it. Whether or not Edward was publicly married to Elizabeth in Westminster Abbey is uncertain, but an ancient manuscript in Corpus Christi College, Cambridge, mentioned by Matthew Parker, supports it. Elizabeth Woodville was crowned with magnificence on Whit Sunday, 26th May 1465 in the Abbey by Thomas Bouchier. The King's younger brother George, Duke of Clarence, held the office of high steward at this ceremony; Shakespeare's "false, fleeting, perjured Clarence". Among the honoured guests was her uncle, Jacques of Luxembourg, nicknamed "Lord Jakes" by the Londoners. After the coronation, Elizabeth haughtily sat in her state chair at the banquet in Westminster Hall. The Bishop of Rochester, who had sung the Mass at her consecration, was on Edward IV's right hand, while the Duke of Buckingham, now married to the Queen's sister Katherine Woodville, sat on the King's left.

Edward's Queen had closer associations with Westminster Abbey than the King, for she was twice compelled to seek sanctuary within its precincts, receiving there, perhaps, a much needed lesson in humility. The first occasion was in 1470, when Edward had been temporarily forced to fly into exile. Together with her small daughter Elizabeth, another daughter and Lady Scrope, she was the guest of Dr Thomas Millyng, Abbot of Westminster since 1469, who five years later was appointed Bishop of Hereford. Millyng had Yorkish sympathies and proved himself a good friend to the Queen in these desperate days. What a contrast to five years ago when her baby Elizabeth had been baptised with much pomp in Westminster Abbey. It had been a lovely scene when the lights of a thousand candles played strange tricks of light against the tapestries on the walls. The Queen's mother, Jacqueline, Duchess of Bedford, and the King's mother Cecily, Duchess of York, were the godmothers, and the Earl of Warwick the godfather. The Queen lived in a room of the Abbot's house at Cheyneygates, working at her embroidery and studying the illuminations in the books of Abbot Millyng's library. While in sanctuary on 3rd November 1470, Elizabeth gave birth to a son, who was christened Edward in the Abbey. This Prince, the future Edward V, was not destined to be crowned king. A local Westminster butcher William Gould sent half a beef and two muttons every week to the royal fugitives. Edward IV later wrote to thank the man for his trouble. Millyng, too, was solicitous, providing the Queen and her children with sweets, cloth and books.

It was Millyng, a most conscientious Abbot, who supervised the continuation of the work of the nave. This had ceased when the infant Henry VI ascended the throne. King Edward was so appreciative of Millyng's part in succouring his Queen that he gave him £520 which was used to roof in one bay of the nave.

Millyng's successor, Abbot Esteney, also a Yorkish sympathizer, was William Caxton's patron. The great printer, related to one of the monks Richard Caxton, first set up his printing press within the precincts of the Abbey near the almonry in 1476. It was here that Caxton published the earliest printed book in England, called *The Game of Chess*. His first patrons were Elizabeth's brother Anthony Woodville and Tiptoft, Earl of Worcester, a curious blend of deep culture and cruelty, for he was known as 'the butcher'.

Edward landed at Ravenspur in March 1461, marched south and the Tower with the royal Henry VI surrendered to him. Edward hurried to Westminster Abbey, eager once again to see his Queen and children, prayed there awhile, and was soon reunited with Elizabeth in Westminster Palace. After he had defeated the Lancastrians and Warwick at the Battle of Barnet (1471) and won the Battle of Tewkesbury against Queen Margaret (1473), when her son Prince Edward was killed, Edward IV felt more secure in his kingdom.

We hear of Edward attending an impressive service in Westminster Abbey during 1471-1472. It was then that a distinguished Burgundian, Louis de Bruges, Seigneur de Gruthuyse, who had befriended Edward in times of adversity, visited the King at Windsor. To honour him in London, Edward dressed in a robe of cloth of gold with a lining of scarlet satin, heading a procession to the Abbey.

Edward died in Westminster Palace on 9th April 1483, and his body was borne into the abbey of Westminster. The resplendent canopy of scarlet cloth, imperial fringed with blue and gold silk was carried aloft by four knights, and behind them came four others holding the banners of the Holy Trinity, the Virgin Mary, St George and St Edward. Then the bier was placed in a hearse, and the melancholy procession continued its journey to Windsor, where it is more fitting than the 'White Rose of Rouen' should be buried than at Westminster, for he founded St George's Chapel just over four hundred years ago.

Several courtiers and officials of St Edward's Court are, however, buried in the Abbey – among them Sir Thomas Vaughan, his Treasurer, and Humphrey Bourchier, who was killed at Barnet, and buried in St Edmund's Chapel. Westminster Abbey also claimed Lord Carew.

How appropriate it is that the eminent Victorian novelist

Edward Bulmer-Lytton author of *Last of the Barons*, the story of Richard Neville, Earl of Warwick, the king-maker who put Edward IV on the throne, should be buried in St Edmund's Chapel near the courtiers of that same king.

By his testament Edward IV had appointed his younger surviving brother, Richard Duke of Gloucester, Protector of the Realm during his son Edward's minority. It is obvious that during the next few weeks the Queen Mother and her kindred the Woodvilles, ignored Richard's appointment as Lord Protector. They incessantly intrigued to get power into their own hands. They conspired against Richard. Then Robert Stillington, Bishop of Bath and Wells, who hated the Woodvilles, came forward with the dramatic disclosure that Edward V and his younger brother Richard Duke of York, had no rightful claim to the throne, since Elizabeth Woodville had not been Edward's lawful wife. There was evidence to prove that there had been a pre-contract to the Lady Eleanor Butler, a lady, who had died in 1468. This pre-contract of marriage is mentioned in the contemporary Croyland Chronicle.

The Tudor historians have stigmatized Richard III as a monstrous hunchback, a bloodthirsty tyrant and a scheming usurper, but a dispassionate study of what is known of his real character reveals that the image has been exaggerated. This last of the Plantagenet kings is a tragic, essentially lonely personality, as Paul Murray Kendall maintains in his biography *Richard the Third*. It may well be that Richard had his nephews murdered in the Tower, but the fate of 'the little Princes', now buried in Westminster Abbey remains a baffling mystery. It is just as likely that Edward V and his brother were murdered by Henry Stafford, second Duke of Buckingham, whether or not with Richard's connivance is not clear. Richard was a ruthless, hard man and in that brutal age he had need of those qualities. Richard's elder brother George, Duke of Clarence, had been attainted during Edward IV's reign and died mysteriously in the Tower, so his son, the Earl of Warwick, had no right to the Crown. Richard was offered the throne by a great assembly of nobles and citizens of London at Baynard's Castle, a house on the Thames which belonged to his mother the old Duchess of York, 'the Fair Rose of Raby'. Richard then rode, on 26th June 1483, at the head of a splendid train to Westminster Hall where he seated himself on the marble chair of King's Bench. Afterwards he entered the Abbey to make his offerings at the Shrine of Edward the Confessor.

Richard's coronation on 6th July, with his Queen Anne Neville, a daughter of the great king-maker Richard, Earl of Warwick, was one of the most magnificent ever to take place in Westminster Abbey. The Duke of Buckingham, who had helped Richard to the throne, insisted on taking the chief part in the enthroning ceremony, though it was the traditional right of the Earl Marshals. John Howard, Duke of Norfolk, had been created High Steward of England for the ceremony, and must have been incensed that Buckingham had been set over him as first officer of the coronation. Buckingham, handsome, vain and eloquent as Clarence had once been, wore a gown of blue velvet aglow with a design of golden cartwheels. Richard himself wore a long gown of purple velvet, furred with ermine. Among the Harleian MSS there is an order to "Piers Curtseys" to deliver for the use of the Queen "four and a half yard of purpille cloth of gold upon damask".

In the procession, the Duke of Norfolk carried the King's crown before him, while the Duke of Buckingham with a white staff in his hand bore Richard's train. The Earl of Huntingdon bore the Queen's sceptre, Viscount Lisle the rod with the dove, and the Earl of Wiltshire her crown. The pious Margaret Beaufort, Countess of Richmond, Lord Stanley's wife and Henry Tudor's mother, had the honour of bearing the Queen's train. Over Anne's head was held a canopy, and "on her head a circlet of gold, with many precious stones set therein" (according to the Harleian MSS). So Richard and Anne walked from St Edward's Shrine to the high altar. Then, after being partly undressed and naked to the waist, they were anointed with the sacred ointment. They were next dressed in cloth of gold, and the learned Cardinal Bourchier, who had crowned Edward IV, set crowns upon their heads. A wonderful spectacle enhanced by the beauty of the music.

At the coronation banquet in Westminster Hall, the Lord Mayor served the royal couple with wafers, hippocras and sweet wine. The darkness of a summer night had descended and attendants hurriedly entered, carrying wax torches and wax torchets. The lords and ladies then made their obeisance to the new sovereigns. While they were at dinner, the King's Champion Sir Robert Dymoke rode into the hall, arrayed in white armour, and made his customary challenge. Then the hall rang with shouts of "King Richard, King Richard".

There is every reason to believe that Richard was genuinely attached to his wife Anne Neville. He had known her in the early days at Middleham Castle in Wensleydale, Yorkshire and they had been happy together. The death of their son Edward was a bitter blow. Both the king-maker's daughters were delicate, Isabella the more beautiful of the two, who married "false, fleeting, perjured Clarence", and is buried with her husband in Tewkesbury Abbey. Anne died at Westminster Palace on 16th March 1485 during a great eclipse of the sun. She is buried in Westminster Abbey in front of the sedilia. Richard's tears at her funeral were not feigned, for he sincerely regretted the passing of the gentle Anne.

During 1483, Queen Elizabeth Woodville was again in sanctuary in Westminster Abbey, together with her younger son Richard, Duke of York, who was aged nine. He was married in childhood to the Lady Anne Mowbray, daughter of John Duke of Norfolk. The pathetic child, however, died in 1481 and lay in state in the Jerusalem Chamber. She was first buried in the now destroyed Chapel of St Erasmus in Westminster Abbey. The coffin containing her skeleton was discovered in 1964 by workmen digging on the site of the Abbey of the Minoresses of St Clare in Stepney. It seems that her coffin had evidently been transferred to the nunnery in 1502 when St Erasmus's Chapel was demolished in order to make way for Henry VII's Chapel. At a simple private ceremony on 31st May 1965, attended by Lord Mowbray, and others when Dr Eric Abbot, Dean of Westminster officiated, Anne Mowbray was reburied in Henry VII's Chapel.

The Council, however, insisted that Richard be withdrawn from sanctuary, and the boy rejoined his brother in the Tower. Elizabeth's five daughters were also with her in the Abbey, near the chapter house where the Commons assembled for their sessions. It was in 1484 that Richard managed to persuade "Elizabeth Grey, late calling herself Queen of England" to allow her daughters to come out of sanctuary, promising them their safety and that they would not suffer any hurt under his protection. It was John Esteney, Abbot of Westminster, who once again entertained Elizabeth Woodville, and it was his pleasure to give her hospitality in the Abbot's house, Cheyneygates, after Bosworth, when she regained the full rights of Queen-dowager in 1486.

Richard III was responsible at least for one building at Westminster – a stone gateway, standing at the north-western extremity of the Palace demesne, which almost directly faced the gate of the Abbey Sanctuary. He was generous, too, in his contributions of 250 marks for continuing Edward IV's work in the building of St George's Chapel, Windsor, and £300 donated for the building of King's College Chapel, Cambridge.

In the depths of his agony after Anne's death, Richard, obsessed with the longing for an heir, may have played with the idea of marrying Princess Elizabeth of York, his own niece, destined to marry Henry Tudor and to unite the white and red roses.

Buckingham headed a rebellion against King Richard in 1483, but was captured and beheaded as a traitor in the market place of Salisbury. Richard himself, as is well known, died later bravely fighting for his life on Bosworth field, crying "Treason, Treason" as Stanley's troops turned against him. His body, hideously disfigured, was carried upon a packhorse to be buried without a monument in the hospitable house of the Grey Friars at Leicester. In such a way did our first Tudor sovereign ascend the throne rather by right of conquest than by hereditary right as Henry VII.

BIBLIOGRAPHY

Brayley and Britton, *Ancient Palace at Westminster* (1836)
Earle, Peter, *The Life and Times of Henry V* (1972)
Ellis, Henry, (ed.) *Original Letters Illustrative of English History*, series 2.I
    London (1825-1846)
Harleian Mss. British Museum. MS 2215
Hutchinson, Harold F., *Henry V, a Biography* (1967)

Hook, Walter Farquahar, *Lives of the Archbishops of Canterbury* Vol. 5 (1860-1884)
Kendall, Paul Murray, *Richard III* (1955)
Ross, Charles, *Edward IV* (1974)
Simons, Eric N., *The Reign of Edward IV*
Wylie, James Hamilton, *The Reign of Henry V* Vols I & II (1919)

6

The Tudors and the Abbey

It would hardly be expected that Henry Tudor – now Henry VII
– would be well disposed towards Abbot Esteney, the Yorkist.
Nor did he favour the sanctuary men, and he took the
opportunity of fining the Abbey a thousand marks after he heard
that twelve prisoners had escaped from the Abbot's prison at
Westminster. It was Eastney who once again entertained Queen
Elizabeth Woodville in the Abbot's house, Cheyneygates, when
her full rights as Queen-dowager had been restored to her in
1486 by Henry VII. She retired to the convent of Bermondsey
where she died in 1492, and was interred in the tomb of Edward
IV in St George's Chapel Windsor.

The coronation of Henry VII was a very sober affair compared
with the magnificence of his predecessor King Richard's
crowning. For the third time decrepit Archbishop Bourchier
crowned a King in Westminster Abbey, but most of the
elaborate ritual was supervised by the Lancastrian Bishops
Morton of Ely and Courtenay of Exeter.

Henry, who certainly liked display, wore a doublet of cloth of
gold and white and green satin, the Tudor colours. Over his
doublet was "a large gowne of purpure velvet, furred with
ermyne, laced with gold and with tasselles of Venys gold, with a
rich sarpe (collar or scarf) and garter".

It was now that the 'Yeomen of the Guard' (of the body of)
the King appeared at Westminster Abbey, selected for their
loyalty. They were a permanent personal bodyguard like those
who attended the French King. When they dined together they
had a reputation for good food, which may be the origin of the
term 'Beefeaters".

Lord Stanley, Lord High Steward, now Earl of Derby,

husband of the King's mother Lady Margaret Beaufort, carried the King's sword, while Henry's uncle, Jasper, created Duke of Bedford, bore the crown, and the Earl of Essex the King's spurs. Spectators noticed that the Lady Margaret "wept marvellously", and one can only assume that this lady's suppressed feelings at last found an outlet. During the banquet in Westminster Hall, Sir Robert Dymoke again appeared as the King's Champion. Ironically enough he had performed the same function at Richard III's coronation, riding into the hall on his magnificent horse.

Henry's marriage on 18th January 1486 at Westminster to Elizabeth of York was a much more splendid ceremony that his coronation. From her effigy in Westminster Abbey and from her portraits, it is clear that Elizabeth was beautiful, having a fair complexion and long golden hair. She was rather tall. She must have been very familiar with the Abbey, having known it whilst in sanctuary with her mother in the early days.

What kind of man was Henry, this man partly Welsh, who built his palace on the old site of the Palace at Sheen and called it Richmond? Before his accession he had been Earl of Richmond, the Yorkshire honour. Henry's parsimonious nature has been stressed too much, while little has been said about his delight in organizing entertainments for his guests. He spent as much as £14,000 per annum on lavish hospitality. He kept up a show of royal state to impress his contemporaries. He loved fine clothes and jewels. Ambassadors wrote of Henry wearing violet-coloured gowns lined with cloth of gold, and a collar of many jewels in his cap.

He has been overshadowed by the more flamboyant personality of Henry VIII. It intrigued me whilst serving in Westminster Abbey, that our visitors were interested in the son, not the father, despite the marvels of the Henry VII Chapel, which drew its inspiration from the King. "Is Henry VIII buried here?" they would ask me. "No, he lies in St George's Chapel, Windsor with his favourite wife Jane Seymour," I would tell them.

There was much of the Welshman in Henry VII, as Francis Bacon wrote of him at Gorhambury in his last years: "He was a prince, sad and serious, and full of thoughts and memorials of his own, especially touching persons." Suspicious, secretive, distrustful, so that he employed "flies and familiars" to investigate plots, Henry reminds one of a churchman, tight-lipped and very subtle. He kept his own accounts, for which he has been derided. In modern times he would have made a shrewd merchant banker, for he was a brilliant financier. A man of Henry's character is seldom loved, but he is feared and respected.

The original purpose of the Henry VII Chapel was as the burial place of Henry VI, whose body it was planned to bring to Westminster from Windsor. If the Pope were to consent, Henry wanted his namesake to be canonized. It was also intended that the Chapel should contain the tombs of Elizabeth of York and the King himself. The Henry VII Chapel was dedicated to the Virgin Mary, to whom the King was especially devoted.

It was on 24th January 1503 that the first stone of the new Chapel was laid by Abbot Islip of Westminster, Sir Reginald Bray and others. The architect of the Chapel is now considered to be Robert Vertue, while William Bolton, Prior of St Bartholomew's Smithfield, was the master of the works. To build the new work it was necessary to demolish the original Lady Chapel of Henry III, and the St Erasmus Chapel built by Queen Elizabeth Woodville as a token of gratitude for the hospitality of the abbots and monks of Westminster. The first person to be buried there was Elizabeth of York. Until more progress could be made with the erection of the new chapel, she was interred in one of the side chapels.

She had died in the Tower on 11th February, the last Queen of England to use the Tower as a place of residence. Thirty-seven virgins, corresponding with Elizabeth's age, all wearing white and green and bearing lighted tapers, stood in Fenchurch and Cheapside. At the funeral in Westminster Abbey, Elizabeth's sister Katharine was the chief mourner. Even as the Plantagenet kings deteriorated in character after the death of their queens, so did Henry VII after Elizabeth's death. He became more avaricious and close-fisted.

Henry VII was on friendly terms with John Islip, Abbot of Westminster, who had succeeded George Fascet as Abbot in 1500. Islip, born in the village of that name in Oxfordshire, was among the greatest of the abbots. His household accounts among the Abbey muniments show that the King occasionally dined with Islip at the Manor of Cheyneygates (the name is derived

from the French word *chêne*, an oak). Islip's cook was renowned
for the excellence of his marrow-bone puddings. On Friday 11th
June 1501, when Henry dined with the Abbot, no meat was
naturally served, but wine and strawberries together cost 3s. 8d.,
and a barrel of ale 2s. The King created Islip a Privy Counsellor,
and he also later served Henry VIII in that capacity. From 1501
onwards Henry VII gave Islip a yearly present of two tuns of
wine. According to Richard Widmore, Islip was the treasurer or
paymaster for the Henry VII Chapel. About ten days before his
death·in 1509, the King sent the Abbot five thousand pounds, so
that the Chapel could be finished. The expenses amounted
altogether to £14,000. The stone used for the building came
from Huddleston Quarry in Yorkshire.

It was Abbot Islip who built the Jesus Chapel, now known as
the Islip Chapel or Chantry. Today it is also the nurses' chapel.
He was also responsible for the reconstruction of the buildings on
the north side of the Abbot's courtyard, and for part of the work
of the Jericho Parlour with its beautiful panelling, together with
the rooms above. Laurence Tanner, former keeper of the
muniments, relates that it was Dean Lancelot Andrewes (a great
preacher) who provided the panelling in the room immediately
above the Jericho Parlour.

Nobody who enters the Henry VII Chapel can fail to be
inspired by its Gothic architecture. With its wonderful fan-
vaulted roof, its exquisite stalls of the Knights of the Bath, with
their gay and colourful banners, and its imposing tombs, it is
undoubtedly one of the Abbey's greatest attractions. When we
contemplate its wonders, let us remember that it took sixteen
years to complete. As Francis Bond wrote of it: "It is far in
advance of anything of contemporary date in England, or France
or Italy or Spain. It shews us Gothic architecture not sinking into
senile decay, as some have idly taught, but bursting forth
phoenix-like, into new life, instinct with the freshness and
originality of youth."

Henry VI's body was never removed to Westminster Abbey
from Windsor, though both the Abbeys of Westminster and
Chertsey contested Windsor's claim to the royal corpse. At the
judicial inquiry in 1498, Westminster was represented by George
Fascet, then the Prior, and John Islip the monk-bailiff, who

possessed legal training. The case was decided in favour of Westminster, but the translation never took place. It is unfortunate, though Windsor could at least claim that Henry had been born there, and that they actually possessed the King's body. It was argued on behalf of the Abbey of Chertsey that Richard III had removed the saintly King's body by violence to Windsor.

It was fitting enough that Henry VII should die at Richmond Palace on 21st April 1509. From Richmond the funeral procession came to St Paul's, where Fisher, Bishop of Rochester, preached the sermon. Then on to Westminster Abbey where Fitzjames, Bishop of London, performed a like function. Archbishop Warham officiated, Henry was buried in the cavernous vault by the side of his consort, Elizabeth of York, Warham casting in the earth. In Francis Bacon's words, the King "lieth buried at Westminster in one of the stateliest and daintiest monuments of Europe, both for the Chapel and the sepulchre. So that he dwelleth more richly dead, in the monument of his tomb, than he did alive in Richmond or any of his palaces".

It was Henry VII, who was anxious that the great Florentine sculptor Pietro Torrigiano, born in 1472, should come to England to work on the erection of the effigies and the monument. He had made provisions to this effect in his will. Torrigiano had studied under Ghirlandaio, and his early patron was Lorenzo de'Medici. For a time Torrigiano lived in the precincts of the Abbey. The tomb was completed by the Italian in 1518, after six years work. As he was a boastful, quarrelsome man, it is likely that his colleagues found him difficult to collaborate with. The biographer Georgio Vasari mentions his choleric and ungovernable temper, and contemporaries have even described him as a brutal and overbearing man. This shows at least the necessity of divorcing the man from the artist. Vasari relates that Torrigiano, when a student in Florence, was so jealous of Michelangelo Buonarotti that he struck the young genius so hard with his fist that he broke it. Rather than face the wrath of Lorenzo the Magnificent, who especially favoured Michelangelo, Torrigiano fled from Florence. He distinguished himself as a soldier fighting for his native city against Pisa.

For the tomb of Henry VII and Elizabeth of York, a sum of

Elizabeth Woodville, Edward IV's Queen, by an unknown artist

Elizabeth I in her coronation robes, by Guillim Stretes

£1,500 was provided for materials and labour. At the beginning of his reign, Henry VIII planned the building of a chapel for himself and his Spanish Queen, Katharine of Aragon, which was to exceed in grandeur that of his father, and cost £2,000. This project never came into being. Torrigiano was to have carved the effigies. Few people have taken the trouble to follow the career of this extraordinary man. He moved to Spain where he continued to create crucifixes of exquisite beauty near Seville. Denounced by one of his patrons as a heretic, the wretched man was thrown into prison where he committed suicide in 1522.

Undoubtedly Torrigiano's finest work is of the Lady Margaret Beaufort's tomb. She was Countess of Richmond and Derby, and she possessed great influence with her son Henry VII. She died three months after him at the Abbot's house Cheyneygates. There the mother of our first Tudor King lies in the Mary Queen of Scots Chapel with her hands raised in prayer. The Lady Margaret was a patroness of William Caxton, and in a very special way identified with Westminster, for she not only contributed to the endowment of her son's new Chapel, but established charities of her own in connection with it. She was warmly attached to John Fisher, later Bishop of Rochester, whose early career she had helped, and it was he who encouraged the Lady Margaret to found Christ's College, Cambridge in 1505, and after her death St John's College – another project dear to Lady Margaret's heart. Fisher was later to suffer for his courage in daring to challenge the royal supremacy of Henry VIII.

There is interred in St Paul's Chapel, Henry VII's Lord Chamberlain, Giles Lord Daubeny, formerly Esquire to the Body of Edward IV and Constable of Bristol Castle. He came of an ancient Norman family and lies in an altar tomb of Purbeck marble. The iron grille which once surrounded the monument has been replaced by a modern one. He died in 1508 and his wife Elizabeth, daughter of Sir John Arundel of Lanherne, Cornwall lies by his side.

Henry VII's eldest son Arthur had died at Ludlow, and he was succeeded by Henry VIII, then a prince of magnificent physique and extremely handsome, not quite eighteen. Together with his Queen, Katharine of Aragon, he was crowned in Westminster Abbey on 24th June 1509, by Archbishop Warham. For the

Londoners the pageantry seemed to herald a golden age. On the eve of their coronation the King and Queen went in procession from the Tower. The King was richly dressed in crimson velvet furred with ermine, and sparkling with rubies, emeralds, diamonds and pearls. The city was gay with decorations, particularly the goldsmiths' stalls in Old Change lively with girls in white waving branches of may.

On this day of high summer, Henry's Queen, daughter of Ferdinand of Aragon, and Isabella of Castile, looked very elegant and pretty. In her white satin dress, her long golden brown hair flowing over her shoulders, she was borne in her litter between two white palfreys, her serious grey eyes glancing appraisingly here and there. King Harry and not forgotten his old nurse Anne Luke, for she was given a place in the Abbey as one of Queen Katharine's Chamber Women.

Afterwards the coronation banquet in Westminster Hall was "greater than any Caesar had known". Among those who played an important part was Edward Stafford, third Duke of Buckingham, appointed Lord High Steward for the coronation, even as his father had once officiated as Great Chamberlain at Richard III's coronation. Because of his high birth and arrogant pretensions, Buckingham was to incur King Henry's jealousy and to be executed some twelve years later. He is Shakespeare's Buckingham in *Henry VIII*, and the lovely poetry makes us pity that nobleman, even if he was a foolish, misguided man, as he kneels on the scaffold:

> Go with me, like good angels to my end;
> And, as the long divorce of steel falls on me,
> Make of your prayers one sweet sacrifice
> And lift my soul to heaven.

Abbot Islip was not on the same intimate terms with Henry VIII as he had been with his father. However, he was both active as a Privy Counsellor and in the House of Lords. Henry also employed him in various diplomatic functions, such as helping to entertain the French diplomats during the summer of 1520 when they were shown the sights of London. On this occasion he entertained the three gentlemen, who composed the mission with "right, goodly chere", showing them the King's new Chapel at Westminster.

He was on friendly terms with Cardinal Wolsey in the days of his greatness. When Wolsey visited Westminster Abbey in January 1519, giving the Abbot official notice when he was coming, Islip and his monks were present in the chapter house. Occasionally Islip presided here at the trials of heretics, and Cardinal Wolsey himself presided at the trial of Thomas Bilney, described in Foxe's *Book of Martyrs*.

During his abbacy, Islip held fast to the rights of sanctuary for those who sought shelter within the Abbey walls. Among them was John Skelton, the Poet Laureate, who fiercely attacked Cardinal Wolsey in satirical verses such as "Why Come ye Not to Courte?" After the dissolution of the Abbey, the rights of the sanctuary were dissolved. Sanctuary for treason, however, was abolished in 1534, while that for debt remained a privilege until the last years of James I. So long as Islip lived, he refused to concede that Wolsey had the right to interfere in matters of sanctuary.

With the downfall of the Cardinal in October 1529, Islip's own position was in jeopardy. He managed, however, to retain the King's precarious favour, and was forced to acquiesce when Henry seized the opportunity of despoiling the Abbey of its houses in Whitehall. In exchange, Henry presented the Abbey with the Priory of Poughley in Berkshire, which was worth far less. During his last years Islip made use of his administrative ability in collaborating with Henry's new minister Thomas Cromwell, who received a bribe from the Abbey under the guise of an annual payment.

As he lay dying at his Manor House of La Neyte on Sunday, 12th May 1532, Abbot Islip must have been aware of the approaching doom of the Abbey of Westminster. Islip was given a magnificent funeral and his body interred in his own little Chapel, then the Jesus Chapel, "The corps covered with a rich pall of cloth of gold tyshew, and burning day and night four great tapers."

Islip was succeeded during 1533 as Abbot of Westminster by the obsequious monk William Boston or Benson, born in Boston in Lincolnshire, selected by the tyrannical Henry VIII for his high position where preceding abbots had always been chosen from its own chapter. He may have been a native of Peterborough, according to Westlake. If so, the place name of Boston is difficult to explain. A servile and scheming place-seeker, he had ingratiated himself with his master by voting against the validity of Henry VIII's marriage to Katharine of Aragon.

Henry VIII was privately married to Anne Boleyn in early 1533. She has the distinction of being the only one of Henry's wives to be crowned alone in Westminster Abbey. It was a day of triumph for this clever, attractive woman, and Henry's love letters, now in the Vatican, reveal that he had been passionately in love with her. Before her coronation Anne spent two days in the Tower when sixty-three knights received the accolade and eighteen Knights of the Bath were created.

For her coronation on Sunday 1st June, Anne wore a robe of purple velvet trimmed with ermine. From Westminster Hall the procession formed to escort the Queen to the Abbey, her train carried by the Dowager Duchess of Norfolk, and the Bishops of London and Winchester walking each side of her holding up "the laps of her robe". The Abbot and monks of Westminster were there in their rich copes. The crown was borne before her by the bovine but handsome Charles Brandon, Duke of Suffolk, the King's intimate friend and brother-in-law, who had formerly opposed the marriage. Henry's youngest sister, Mary, Duchess of Suffolk (she had been Queen of France) was not present for she lay mortally ill in Suffolk. Under a canopy borne by four Knights of the Cinque Ports, Anne entered the Abbey. What an ordeal for Henry's new Queen, who was five months with child, even if her mind was filled with elation as she gazed at the female nobility of England in their scarlet surcoats. The Archbishop of Canterbury, Thomas Cranmer, anointed her on the head and temples at the High Altar. Then the heavy Crown of St Edward was set on her head, and then a lighter one. How merciful it is that most people are not gifted to see the future. It was only a brief, gaudy hour of triumph for this ambitious woman, destined to be mother of our greatest Queen, although she knew how desperately Henry longed for a male heir. Her right hand held the golden sceptre, her left the rod of ivory with the dove, symbols of mercy and power.

During the banquet in Westminster Hall the Duke of Suffolk rode about the Hall, his horse richly caparisoned in scarlet, escorting the server and the Knights of the Bath, who bore a dish of the first course for the Queen's table. Henry took no part in the ceremonial, watching it from a latticed closet of the Cloister of St Stephen's together with the Venetian and French ambassadors.

The years 1533-1540 when the medieval monasteries throughout England were dissolved, were tragic years for the Abbey of Westminster. Boston anxious to please the rapacious Thomas Cromwell, granted him the office of Janitor of the Monastery and Keeper of the Gatehouse Prisons, also that of Seneschal and Steward. Cromwell appointed a deputy. During these desperate times there were statesmen and clerics brave and steadfast enough to refuse to acknowledge the despotic Henry as supreme head of the Church, and they were to die for their faith. Such were Sir Thomas More and Bishop Fisher of Rochester. On refusing the Oath of Supremacy in 1534, More was in the custody of the Abbot of Westminster for four days, who in his craven way did his best to make Sir Thomas bow to the prevailing wind "and change my consciens", as he wrote to his daughter Margaret Roper.

It was in the chapter house during Boston's abbacy that the reading of the Comperta or findings of the commissioners, appointed to provide a case against the monasteries of England, took place.

During September 1533, Boston assisted at the christening of Henry's and Anne's infant daughter, Princess Elizabeth. Instead of resisting the King's greedy demands the Abbot was only too ready to comply with them, exchanging valuable property in Westminster itself, and the Manors of Neyte and other places for the Priory of Hurley in Berkshire and various land of much less value. In one matter Boston remained steadfast, defending the rights of sanctuary at St Martin-le-Grand against the growing pressure of the Corporation of London. Otherwise he is the servile servant, presiding at the chapter house on 16th January 1540, when the Deed of Surrender was signed by twenty-four monks putting an end to the Abbey at Westminster. In December the town of Westminster became a city and the Abbey

Church temporarily a cathedral. A favourite of Cranmer's, Thomas Thirby, was consecrated by Bonner, Bishop of London and Ridley, Bishop of Rochester as Westminster's first Bishop.

Boston now became Dean Benson, and he proved more conscientious and hard-working in this capacity than as Abbot. Benson died in September 1549 during the short reign of Henry's son Edward VI, whose health was very feeble. Benson's successor Dr Richard Cox, an Etonian and Fellow of King's College, Cambridge was installed as Dean. He was on friendly terms with the boy King, and no doubt influenced him in his staunch protestantism. Richard Cox was to later fall foul of Mary Tudor as he was implicated in John Dudley, the Duke of Northumberland's plot on behalf of his daughter-in-law Lady Jane Grey.

Edward VI, son of Henry VIII by his third Queen, Jane Seymour, succeeded his father in early 1547 on his death in the Palace of Westminster. The King was short, had a fair complexion and his eyes were weak. He suffered from periodical deafness. This precocious, priggish boy is not altogether a sympathetic character, especially when we consider his callous behaviour before his uncle the Duke of Somerset's execution. Edward's health was very delicate. Somerset, now Protector of the Realm and the Duke of Northumberland, influenced the boy King's religious sentiments by surrounding him with puritans.

Edward's coronation was arranged for Shrove Tuesday 20th February. Stanley relates that an Aragonese sailor during the procession to the Abbey capered on a tight-rope down from the battlements of St Paul's to a window at the Dean's gate, an antic which delighted Edward. One innovation was that the King was not met at the Abbey door by the Abbot or Dean, but by the Bishop of Westminster. He was seated on Edward the Confessor's chair, while the Duke of Somerset held the crown. It was set on the King's head by Thomas Cranmer, Archbishop of Canterbury. Actually, Cranmer placed three crowns in succession on the King's head, the Confessor's, the Imperial and one which had been made especially for the occasion. Cranmer, Edward's godfather, now delivered an address, explaining to him the nature of his coronation oath, and its significance. Cranmer acknowledged Edward as the supreme head of the

Church, for the See of Rome was not the arbiter of his right to rule.

Edward VI died peacefully in the arms of his chief attendant, Sir Henry Sidney in 1553. Unlike his father and mother, Edward, aged only sixteen, was buried in the Henry VII Chapel. It was now that the Burial Service of the English prayer book was used for the first time over a sovereign at his funeral. The chief mourner was Lord Treasurer, the Marquis of Winchester, and the cost of the ceremony amounted to £5,946. 9s. 9d. Edward's half-sister Mary, daughter of Henry VIII and Katharine of Aragon, was absent from the Abbey, but attended a Requiem Mass sung in the Tower.

The Duke of Northumberland's plot to place his daughter-in-law Lady Jane Grey on the throne, was frustrated by the papist Queen Mary, who showed something of the courage and firmness of purpose of her father at this juncture. Her standard was raised at Framlingham Castle in Suffolk, Northumberland was arrested and executed in the Tower of London.

Mary was short, sandy-haired, deep-voiced and had the fiery temper of the Tudors. She was, like her half-sister Elizabeth, the future Queen, a talented musician. She was crowned on 1st October 1558, and in the procession to Westminster Abbey from Westminster Hall, the Queen dressed in her crimson robes, walked under a canopy, borne by the Barons of the Cinque Ports. Following the Queen walked the young Princess Elizabeth, and the Lady Anne of Cleves, Henry VIII's fourth Queen was among those attending the ceremony. Since the Archbishops of Canterbury, and York and the Bishop of London were prisoners in the Tower, Gardiner as Bishop of Winchester officiated without any express right or precedent. He presented her to the people during the recognition part of the ceremony, speaking these words: "Will you serve at this time and give your wills and assent to the same consecration, unction and coronation?" The people answered in unison: "Yea, yea, yea! God Save Queen Mary!" Agnes Strickland describes her seated, dressed "in her royal robes of velvet, a mantle with a train, a surcoat with a kirtle furred with combs of miniver pure; a riband of Venice gold ..."

It may well be that Mary did not sit in the Coronation chair, but the Pope did send for a special chair from Winchester Cathedral, for the Catholic Queen feared that the seat where her half-brother had sat might be polluted. This chair may still be seen in the Cathedral. Princess Elizabeth is said to have complained to the French Ambassador, Noailles of the weight of her coronet. "Have patience," said Noailles, "and before long you will exchange it for a crown." She had indeed only five years to wait, years full of frustration and suspense.

Four days later Queen Mary opened her first Parliament. Dressed in scarlet velvet robes she rode to Westminster Abbey. There was celebrated the Mass of the Holy Ghost, much to the baffled anger of the Bishops of Lincoln and Hereford, both sturdy Protestants. Since they refused to kneel at the Mass, they were violently ejected from the Abbey.

During the summer of 1554, Mary I married Philip II of Spain in Winchester Cathedral, a marriage which was very unpopular with most of her Protestant subjects. The Queen ordered Hugh Weston, Dean of Westminster, to head various religious processions, which marched through London, praying God to grant her the gift of a longed-for son. The Queen was anxious that Weston should make way for her confessor John de Feckenham, and he eventually succeeded Weston as Abbot of Westminster.

Mary's ambition during her short reign was to restore a few of the old religious houses as monasteries, among them the Abbey of Westminster. She was well aware that some of the Benedictine monks desired to re-enter the monastic life. So it transpired that the last years of the ancient Abbey as a Benedictine monastery, so soon to vanish for ever, were not lacking in mystical beauty or in a kind of glory. Today we think mainly of the Marian persecution, the horrible burnings at the stake of the Protestant martyrs such as Bishops Ridley, Latimer and Cranmer.

On 12th November 1554 there was celebrated the Mass of the Holy Ghost at the altar of the Abbey when both Mary and her consort Philip were present. At the forthcoming Parliament it was intended to repeal the attainder of Cardinal Reginald Pole, who had royal blood in his veins. He was about to arrive in England as papal legate on his mission to reunite the Church of

England to the Church of Rome. He was to be a great friend of Westminster Abbey, but he only survived his friend Queen Mary twelve hours. Henry Machyn, a contemporary, describes the scene in his diary. Philip the Spanish King sallying forth from the Holbein gate of Whitehall Palace, attended by six hundred Spanish courtiers, immaculate in their costumes of white velvet, striped with red. It was 30th November, the Feast of St Andrew, the festival of Philip II's highest order, the Golden Fleece. So there took place at this service the reconciliation of the English Church with the See of Rome, which was to prove only temporary, for it was to be reversed when the Protestant Elizabeth succeeded her half-sister in 1558.

Feckenham, last mitred Abbot of Westminster, was a remarkable man and very popular as a preacher. His real name was John Howman, and he took his new name from the Forest of Feckenham in Worcestershire. Feckenham was inclined to stoutness, pleasant and affable in manner and usually good-natured in conversation. Camden describes him as good and erudite, and he was renowned for his charity to the poor. It was a sad blow to him when he failed to convert Lady Jane Grey before her execution. Henry Machyn depicts the scene in the Abbey when Feckenham, late Dean of St Pauls, was installed on 21st November 1556. We can visualize the scene with Machyn's eyes, "the monks in collys (cowls) of black, with vargers (vergers) carehyng sylver rodes (silver rods) in their handes, and at avngsong tyme the vargers whent through the clostur to the Abbot". Are we so removed in time today when the vergers with their maces prepare themselves for Evensong? In his diary, Henry Machyn is so obsessed with funerals that one inclines to the opinion that his profession was an undertaker or furnisher of funerals.

Abbot Feckenham was a staunch champion of the Abbey's right of sanctuary. We hear of him going in a procession with his convent, and "before him went all the sanctuary men". During the same month Queen Mary "rode in her chariot through the Park from Saint James into the Galere, and so (took) her barge into Westmynster, and landyd at the Palace, and so into the Abbey, and then her grace hard (heard) evensong and my lord

Cardenalle (Pole) and my lord Montyguw and my lord Darse of Essex dyd bere the sword a-for her grace, and my lord Montyguw bore up the Queen's train".

On 6th December 1556 the Abbot went in procession with his convent. Before him went all the sanctuary men with cross keys upon their garments. Following them walked three homicides, one of them a nobleman from the north, Lord Dacre, who "was wypyd with a shett (sheet)". The others were the murderer of a tailor in Long Acre, and a small Westminster scholar, who had killed a big boy who "sold papers and pryntyd bokes", by hurling a stone at him and hitting him under his ear in Westminster Hall.

How beautiful and austere the ceremony was when, with a hundred lights, King Edward the Confessor was restored to his original shrine, despoiled by Henry VIII. Machyn's diary relates that the Duke of Muscovy, a diplomat visited it in April 1557 and afterwards dined with the Abbot.

"'The Flanders Mare", as that egotistical King Henry VIII derisively referred to Anne of Cleves, was a kindly and religious lady, who was on friendly terms with Queen Mary and Princess Elizabeth. This fourth Queen of Henry's is the only one to be interred in Westminster Abbey. She died a Roman Catholic convert in 1557 in a house in Chelsea where Sir Thomas More had lived. It was no real misfortune for Anne of Cleves to have her marriage annulled to Henry VIII. How much better treated she was as "his sister" than she would have been as his wife. She is buried in the south side of the High Altar in a vault behind the elaborate chair presented by the Canadian Government to Queen Elizabeth II.

When serving as a temporary marshal, I was sometimes asked where Henry's Queens are buried. Katharine of Aragon is in Peterborough Cathedral, Anne Boleyn in the Tower, Jane Seymour (as already mentioned) with Henry in St George's Chapel, Windsor, Katharine Howard in the Tower and Katharine Parr at Sudely Castle, Gloucestershire.

Henry Machyn gives an account of Anne of Cleves' funeral in August, how her body was borne past St James's Palace and Charing Cross. Bonner, Bishop of London and Feckenham, as Abbot of Westminster, rode together next to the monks. "My

Lord Abbott of Westminster mad a godly sermon as ever was mad, and then ... the Bishop of London sang mass in his myter", the Marchioness of Winchester being the chief mourner. According to Dean Stanley, an artist was brought from Cleves to construct the tomb, but it was Dean Neale in the early reign of James I, who finished the work.

The punishments for criminals were often harsh and brutal. "A pulter's servant, one of them that dyd", who robbed a Spaniard within Westminster Abbey in April 1555, was hung. As the man was on the gallows he railed against the Pope and the Mass. A tall man was whipped in the streets of Westminster and thrown over London Bridge for forging "the master of the Queen's horse's" signature during the third year of Elizabeth's reign.

For most English people, Mary's reign was very unfortunate, and she died unmourned on 17th November 1558. The monks at Westminster were, however, very apprehensive, dreading their future.

The funeral procession passed by Charing Cross and arrived at the great door of Westminster Abbey. Four bishops and the Abbot Feckenham censed the coffin. Mary's corpse was then placed on a hearse, and during the night of 13th December one hundred poor men in good black gowns and hoods on their heads, and carrying long torches watched over her body. When the torches burnt out, wax-chandlers were there to supply others. Mary's obsequies were the last solemnity of the Roman Catholic Church ever to take place in the Abbey with the exception of the Requiem Mass ordered by Queen Elizabeth I a few days later for Charles V, Holy Roman Emperor. The accounts of Sir Edward Waldgrave, Master of the Queen's Great Wardrobe, reveal the curious fact that a drinking for the mourners after the dirge for Charles V and a dinner the following day cost £44. 12s. 3d.

Bishop White of Winchester preached the funeral sermon for Mary's obsequies taking as his text: "A living dog is better than a dead lion." Mary was buried on the north side of Henry VII's Chapel. Today the two half-sisters, Mary and Elizabeth, so antagonistic to one another during their lives, lie side by side.

Elizabeth I succeeded her half-sister at the age of twenty-five. Her genius as a Queen throughout her long reign was her capacity for understanding the feelings of her subjects, an attribute totally lacking in her successor James I. She was proud of her English blood and indeed boasted of it.

Elizabeth was superstitious. Before her coronation she sent her favourite Lord, Robert Dudley to consult the celebrated Dr Dee concerning a propitious day for this important occasion. Dee chose Sunday, 15th January, and the choice of this date was to prove very fortunate. An account in the Mantuan Archives, describes her state entry into London. "The whole Court so sparkled with jewels and gold collars that they cleared the air, though it snowed a little." Her Majesty dressed in a royal robe of very rich cloth of gold, beneath which was her hair. On her head a plain gold crown, covered with jewels and nothing in her hands but gloves. Behind her litter rode the handsome Lord Robert Dudley, Master of the Horse, mounted on a very fine horse, and leading a white hackney covered with cloth of gold. There was the touch of artistry, the instinctive feeling for doing the right thing. An old woman in the crowd tossed a sprig of rosemary upon her lap, whereupon Elizabeth kept the bit of herb in her hand as if it were something precious. In Cheapside somebody shouted: "Remember old King Harry VIII" and a brilliant smile transformed the Queen's face.

Westminster Abbey was decorated with very precious tapestries representing the cartoons of the artist Raphael born in Urbino. These had been bought by Henry VIII. On the Queen's arrival at the Abbey, all the church bells rang. A carpet of purple cloth had been spread for the Queen to walk on. Only Bishop Oglethorpe of Carlisle had agreed to crown Elizabeth, a decision which so pricked his conscience that he soon died of a broken heart. The Queen's long train, her crimson velvet robe was carried by the Duchess of Norfolk, while the Duke of Norfolk, the Lord Marshal, bore the orb. Foreign spectators were impressed by the duchesses, marchionesses and other noble ladies who followed, "exquisitely dressed as they were, with their coronets on their heads, and so handsome and beautiful that it was a marvellous sight".

After she had been anointed, the Queen retired to a side chapel where she changed her crimson robes for gold ones. Bishop Goodman relates in *The Court of James I* that the Queen, who had a fastidious dislike of smells, complained to her ladies "that the oil was grease and smelt ill".

Elizabeth was already very popular. When she came to Westminster for the opening of her first Parliament, the people cried: "God save and maintain thee!" Again identifying herself with her subjects, the Queen answered: "God a' mercy, good people!" One of her actions especially pleased them. When John Feckenham, Abbot of Westminster and his monks greeted her with lighted torches, she exclaimed in her strident voice: "Away with those torches! We see very well."

These were times of adversity for the Marian bishops, such as Edmund Bonner, Bishop of London, who was requested with loving exhortations to surrender the bishopric to "one Master Grindal". A diplomat from Mantua sympathetic to the old religion wrote: "The poor bishop has taken sanctuary in Westminster Abbey to avoid molestation from many persons who demand considerable sums of money from him."

It was Elizabeth, who finally suppressed the monastery of Westminster Abbey during July 1559. Feckenham, who had assisted as a mitred Abbot at Elizabeth's coronation, and all his monks were deprived of their revenues and the remainder of their property. It is related that on ascending to the throne, the Queen had sent for Abbot Feckenham, and her messenger had found him planting elms in the orchard (college garden). Feckenham was of exemplary character, and it may well be that Elizabeth offered the old man the Archbishopric of Canterbury, but he was too honourable a man to accept such an appointment on Elizabeth's conditions. During 1560 he was confined to the Tower, but his imprisonment was not rigorous, and he was a guest later in the custody of Horne, Bishop of Winchester. He died at Wisbech in 1585 and was buried there.

By temperament Elizabeth was religious and she was keenly interested in the Abbey. Almost always before the opening of Parliament, she would visit the Abbey on horseback, entering at the northern door and receiving the sceptre from the Dean. Two important anniversaries were kept, the day of her accession (17th November), and her coronation day (15th January). In place of her father's cathedral and her sister's monastery, Elizabeth instituted the collegiate Church of St Peter, Westminster, under the Dean and twelve prebendaries. William Bill was the first Dean after the new regime had been inaugurated, but he had scarcely completed the collegiate statutes when he died in 1561. He is buried in St Benedict's Chapel. On the other hand, Gabriel Goodman's tenure as Dean lasted forty years, and he was an outstanding one. He was mainly responsible for rehabilitating the Protestant services after the interregnum of Queen Mary's monastery. As mentioned in *A House of Kings*, he carried out a large amount of repair work in the Abbey Church, especially to the bells and organ. His gift of two bells to Westminster is still in use. He was a zealous champion of its rights and privileges. Goodman was held in the highest esteem by Archbishops Parker and Whitgift. In 1590 he founded and endowed a hospital and school at Ruthin in Denbighshire where he was born. In his testament — he died in 1601 — he expressed the wish that the nomination of the warden should be vested in the Dean and Chapter of Westminster.

Queen Elizabeth I was foundress of a great public school, Westminster School, whose links with the Abbey have always remained close. Dean Edward Carpenter is *ex-officio* chairman of the governing body, and frequent services for the boys are held when the Queen's scholars wear white surplices. Since the coronation of James II in 1685, the King's (or Queen's) scholars are present in the Abbey when they acclaim the monarch on entry into the church. To the visitor the schoolboys are a familiar sight as they jostle one another in the sombre cloisters into the Abbey, the air thick with their merry chatter.

Elizabeth appointed her close friend Matthew Parker, Archbishop of Canterbury. He had been chaplain to her mother Anne Boleyn, Elizabeth, however, strongly disapproved of married bishops. On one occasion the Queen ungraciously addressed Archbishop Parker's wife after being magnificently entertained at the archiepiscopal palace: "Madam I may not call you, mistress I am ashamed to call you, and so I know not what to call you, but howsoever, I thank you." Archbishop Parker occasionally reminded the Queen that the conception of a celibate clergy was a Catholic, not a Protestant one.

The reign of Elizabeth I was a period of imposing funerals in

Westminster Abbey. Such was that of Frances Grey, Duchess of Suffolk, daughter of Henry VIII's favourite Charles Brandon, Duke of Suffolk, and Mary, sometime Queen of France. She was mother of the ill-fated Lady Jane Grey. As her second husband, Frances Grey, who was both foolish and tactless, married Adrian Stokes, Esquire. Elizabeth, who disliked her, remarked to somebody: "What, hath she married her horsekeeper?" "Yes, Madam," was the answer, "and she saith that your Majesty would fain do the same," for many courtiers thought Elizabeth was planning to marry her Master of the Horse, Lord Robert Dudley, later Earl of Leicester. There she lies near princes of the blood royal in the Chapel of St Edmund, in a tomb erected by Adrian Stokes.

There is a magnificent monument in St John the Baptist's Chapel, which commemorates Henry Cary, first Baron Hunsdon (died 1596), Queen Elizabeth's first cousin. He was a brave soldier and honourable counsellor, who took a leading part in the suppression of the Catholic Northern rebellion in 1570. Elizabeth was much attached to him, though he found her exasperating. She wrote him the same year: "I doubt much, my Harry, whether that the victory were given me more joyed me, or that you were by God appointed the instrument of my glory." I once showed a visitor from America this monument, who said she was descended from Hunsdon and had come especially to see it.

There is Frances Sidney, Countess of Sussex's monument in the Chapel of St Paul. She was aunt of Sir Philip Sydney, and the second wife of Thomas Ratcliffe, Earl of Sussex, an enemy and rival of the Earl of Leicester. She is celebrated for founding the College of Sidney Sussex in Cambridge, and also another college for the education of clergy of the Church of England. Distinguished Elizabethan Judges have monuments erected to them, such as Sir Thomas Bromley, who presided at the trial of Mary Queen of Scots, and Sir John Puckering, who died in 1596. The marble tomb was erected by his widow, who lies by his side.

Another Elizabethan who had intimate associations with Westminster Abbey, was William Cecil, Lord Burghley, who had in his earlier life lived in the precincts of Westminster. He was a friend of Dean Goodman. The great statesman is not buried in the Abbey, but in St Martin's Church, Stamford, Lincolnshire.

When the old man died, in August, 1598, the Queen had been inconsolable, following the funeral cortège towards Westminster Abbey. His second wife Mildred (Cooke) Lady Burghley, regarded as the most learned woman of her age, lies in the Chapel of St Nicholas. Her grief-stricken husband erected an elaborate monument to commemorate her and their daughter Anne, Countess of Oxford. Other members of the Cecil family who lie in St John the Baptist's Chapel are Thomas Cecil and his first wife Dorothy Neville, daughter of Lord Latimer. Thomas was son of William Cecil by his first marriage to Mary Cheke, and was later created Earl of Exeter by James I. In his early life Sir William Cecil had disapproved of Thomas's "wanton lusts", but he was later described as "right, pious and charitable".

Queen Elizabeth I died on 24th March 1603 in Richmond Palace and her body was borne down the Thames to Westminster Abbey, where she was given a magnificent funeral. Although the nation mourned her loss as a great Queen, her popularity had waned during her last few years, partly owing to the execution of Robert Devereux, Earl of Essex. The funeral sermon was preached by Anthony Watson, Bishop of Chichester. Goodman had been succeeded as Dean of Westminster in July 1601 by Lancelot Andrewes, and he was certainly present on this occasion. The Queen was buried in the north aisle of Henry VII's Chapel in the unmarked grave of her half-sister Mary. It was James I − the first Stuart King of England, who raised a monument over them both.

BIBLIOGRAPHY

Aikin, Lucy, *Court of Elizabeth*, Vol. I (1818)
Bacon, Francis, *The History of the Reign of King Henry the Seventh* (London, The Folio Society 1971)
Bowle, John, *Henry VIII* (1964)
Browning, Andrew, *The Age of Elizabeth*
Butler, Ewan, *The Cecils* (1964)
Chapman, Hester, *Edward VI, The Last Tudor King*
Chrimes, S.B., *Henry VII* (1972)

Halstead, *Lady Margaret Beaufort* (1973)

Harvey, Nancy Lenz, *Elisabeth of York* (1973)

Machyn, Henry, (ed. J. Nichols), *Diary 1550-1563*

Research Citizen and Merchant-Taylor of London from 1550-1563

Garvin, Katharine, *The Great Tudors* (1935)

Abbot Islip's Household Accounts. Muniments 33320 (Westminster Abbey Library)

Jenkins, Elizabeth, *Elizabeth the Great* (1958)

Shakespeare, William, *Henry VIII*

Simons, Eric N., *Henry VII The First Tudor King* (1968)

Storey, R.L., *The Reign of Henry VII* (1968)

Vasari, Georgio, *Le Vite de'piu Eccellente Pittori, Scultori e Architetti* Vol IV.

Williams, Charles, *Henry VII* (1937)

Williams, Neville, *The Life and Times of Henry VII* (1973)

Domestic State Papers, Queen Elizabeth

Venetian State Papers, Queen Mary I

7

Stuart Sovereigns
and Westminster Abbey

James I, the Scottish King, who reigned in England between 1603-1625, was a strange and complex personality. He was gregarious by temperament, but the loneliness of his early life made him distrustful and wary of most people. He was a fair scholar, having a far better brain than his second son Charles who succeeded him. He loathed physical violence. His Scottish sense of humour has been described as homely and pawky. He was a good judge of men, though he made a bad choice of favourites, and on the whole he was just. His greatest failure was his lack of communication with his new subjects, and his absolute inability to understand them. His relationship with his male favourites such as Esme Stuart, Lord of Aubigny, Robert Carr, Earl of Somerset and George Villiers, first Duke of Buckingham were strongly tinged with homosexuality. He could not have been a satisfactory husband for the pleasure-loving, frivolous Anne of Denmark.

The coronation of James and Anne on St James's Day, 25th July 1603 lacked the brilliance and the lustre of most of his predecessors, because plague raged in London. Over 30,000 Londoners died of the pestilence during 1603. Because of this the customary procession from the Tower did not take place. The royal couple, in pouring rain, went straight from Whitehall to Westminster Abbey. Where at the crowning of Elizabeth I – a heretic who succeeded a Catholic Queen – hardly any bishops had been present, a galaxy of bishops attended James's coronation. Archbishop Whitgift crowned James, while Dean Andrewes assisted at the ceremony. It was his duty to hold "the

oyle in a little goulden ladell for the anointing". James's lack of
dignity and want of reverence was much criticized. When the
peers were paying him homage, Philip Herbert, Earl of
Montgomery, the King's handsome favourite, kissed his master
on the cheek, much to the indignation of most of the
congregation. The King, instead of rebuking Montgomery in an
audible whisper, merely laughed and tapped him on the cheek.
Queen Anne, too, was censured for refraining from taking the
Sacrament according to the rites of the Church of England. It was
rumoured that she was popishly inclined. After the coronation
the King and Queen hurriedly moved to Woodstock to escape
the plague.

Lancelot Andrewes was one of the most learned Deans of
Westminster who ever held this office, but he reigned only a
short time. He was a brilliant preacher, a friend of James I,
though never servile to him, and intimate with some of the
leading men of the age, such as Sir Robert Cecil, now High
Steward of Westminster, later Earl of Salisbury, and Sir Francis
Bacon, then rising into prominence. Westminster School owed
much to Dean Andrewes, for he took a great interest in the boys.
He used to invite the older pupils to the Deanery where he held
tutorials.

The great prelate became successively Bishop of Chichester,
then was transferred to Ely and in 1619 to Winchester. He was
indeed expected to succeed Richard Bancroft as Archbishop of
Canterbury, in 1610-1611, but George Abbot, the son of a cloth-
worker in Guildford, received the appointment.

Unlike many of his predecessors, James disliked London "That
filthy Toune". he called it and spent every possible moment out
of the capital. Whilst indulging in his favourite hunting, James
neglected the vital business in his kingdom. A set of doggerel
verses was once found in the hand of Queen Elizabeth I's effigy
on her tomb in Westminster Abbey, comparing the favoured
position of James's hounds with the sorry state of the country.

Roman and Joller, Ringwood and his mate,
Compared to us are in a better state;
They can be heard and they can be regarded,
Where we are lost, slighted and unregarded ...

Richard Neile succeeded Lancelot Andrewes as Dean of Westminster. He had been at Westminster School when the great Camden was headmaster. Neile was a very capable administrator, and during his five years as Dean, he was responsible among other achievements, for repairing the Henry VII Chapel. He also supervised the completion and railing-in of Anne of Cleves' marble tomb.

One of the most magnificent funeral processions ever to take place in the Abbey occurred when Henry, Prince of Wales, a prince of high promise, died prematurely in St James's Palace during the winter of 1612. First came one hundred and forty poor men in gowns. There followed the great standard of Prince Henry borne by Sir John Win. Upon it was embroidered Henry's motto "Fax mentis honestae gloria" – "Glory is the torch which leads on the honourable mind". The young man had a taste for martial prowess and military glory, completely lacking in his father. So, the lugubrious procession wound its slow way to Westminster Abbey, the eighty mourning servants of Archbishop Abbot, of the new heir to the throne Prince Charles, and of the Elector Palatine walking ahead of the aged Lord Howard of Effingham, of Armada fame, who bore the Prince's banner as Earl of Chester. A pathetic mourner sat by his master's coffin Sir David Murray, Henry's most faithful friend and servant. Just before he had died Henry had cried, "David, David, David." The Archbishop of Canterbury conducted the funeral service, and Henry's body was carried to the vault of his grandmother Mary Queen of Scots, who had earlier been transferred to her magnificent tomb in Westminster Abbey from Peterborough Cathedral. It is fascinating, if idle, to speculate what would have happened if Henry had succeeded his father to the throne. Would he have succeeded in building a strong central monarchy such as that achieved by L   XIV? Would he have averted the war between Crown and Parliament? None can say.

James I wrote to the Dean of Peterborough in September 1612, ordering that the body of his mother Mary Queen of Scots should be removed to Westminster Abbey. The two prelates responsible for the removal were the Bishops of Coventry and Lichfield. James's letter can be seen in the Lady Margaret Chapel, which is in the South of the Abbey. Rather naturally James's monument he erected for his mother is finer than the Elizabeth I tomb, but Torrigiano's Lady Margaret Beaufort in the same Chapel excels it in beauty. Such is the magnetism of Mary Queen of Scots, mother of our first Stuart King, that our millions of visitors, attracted by the glamour of her romantic personality, visit her tomb as much as ever.

Another unfortunate lady who is buried in Westminster Abbey, was Lady Arbella Stuart, a cousin of James I. She was daughter of Charles Earl of Lennox, and Elizabeth Cavendish, step-daughter of the Earl of Shrewsbury, under whose custody Mary Queen of Scots spent part of her captivity. Lady Arbella was a typical Stuart, possessing their charm, much of their gaiety and a gift for friendship, but she had a fatal lack of judgement. In 1610 she was rash enough to marry Sir William Seymour (afterwards Marquis of Hertford) without permission, thus incurring the brooding suspicions and jealousy of James. He imprisoned her in the Tower where she died during September 1615. Later James relented so far as to allow Arbella to be interred in the Abbey. According to Dean Stanley, she was brought at midnight by the dark river from the Tower and laid with no solemnity upon the coffin of Mary Stuart. The stealth and secrecy adopted was a complete contrast to Prince Henry's funeral. Her embalmment cost only £6. 13s. 4d.

Two infant children of James I are interred in what Dean Stanley first called Innocents' Corner in the north aisle near to the place where Charles II was later to order the presumed bones of Edward V and Richard Duke of York to be transferred from the Tower. Princess Sophia is sleeping in her alabaster cradle. This monument is by Maximilian Colt. Of her sister Mary, James wittily said, "that he would not pray to the Virgin Mary, but would pray for the Virgin Mary".

According to *A House of Kings*, James's unworthy favourite, Robert Carr, Earl of Somerset, was married to the Lady Frances Howard, the beautiful but depraved niece of Lord Harry Howard (created by James I Earl of Northampton) in December 1613 in Westminster Abbey. Her marriage to Robert Devereux, third Earl of Essex had been annulled. George Mountain, then Dean of Westminster preached in commendation of the young couple. He even praised the bride's rapacious mother, the

Countess of Suffolk, whom he described as "the mother-vine". Ethel Carleton Williams, in her *Anne of Denmark*, states that they were married in the private Chapel or Chapel Royal at Whitehall, which seems more probable. G.R.V. Akrigg also gives the Chapel Royal in his book *Jacobean Pegeant*. As she entered the church with her long golden hair flowing over her shoulders, supported by the Earl of Northampton, she must have been a ravishing sight, but her hair hanging loose would not have deceived many people that she was a virgin. Both the Somersets were deeply involved in a *cause célèbre*, the murder of Sir Thomas Overbury in the Tower, and consequently James was forced to have them tried. Somerset was for a short time in the safe custody of Dean Mountain before being consigned to the Tower.

Archbishop Abbot used his influence at Court with King James and Queen Anne for the promotion of George Villiers (later first Duke of Buckingham) to the post of Gentleman of the Bedchamber. Anne of Denmark with unusual insight warned of the danger: "If this young man be once brought in, the first persons that he will plague must be you that labour for him." However, Anne seems to have got on very well with George Villiers, and referred to him as "My kind dog" and commended him for "lugging the sow's ear", by which she meant that he tried to prevent James's lapses in decorum. Abbot was a conscientious, but not an outstanding Archbishop of Canterbury. He was unfortunate enough to shoot a keeper by accident whilst staying with his friend Lord Zouch in his country home in Hampshire. For a period Abbot thought it wise to retire to the almshouse he had founded at Guildford.

Anne of Denmark at least was fond of the theatre, and had a passion for masques, but she was very extravagant. She predeceased James, dying at Hampton Court in March 1619. James, who had a morbid horror of funerals, did not attend, nor had he been present at his son's. The arrangements were marred by an unseemly quarrel between the Countesses of Nottingham and Arundel, as to who should be the chief mourner. It was also delayed because of lack of money. It took place on 13th May when Prince Charles walked immediately before the hearse and the Marquises of Buckingham and Hamilton, and the Earls of Arundel and others carried the coffin through the west door of

Westminster Abbey. To John Chamberlain, an eyewitness, the funeral was but "a brawling, tedious sight, more remarkable for number than for any other singularity". Abbot, Archbishop of Canterbury preached the funeral sermon. Anne was buried privately in the east end of the Henry VII Chapel at 7 p.m. and only the Dean of Westminster, the prebends and Sir Edward Zouch, the Knight Marshal were present. No monument marked her grave, but today the wax head of this Queen taken from her death mask can be seen in the Norman undercroft.

Far the most important of the Deans of Westminster during the later reign of James I, was the little Welshman, John Williams, who managed to retain the coveted post for twenty-four years. To acquire it, Williams intrigued incessantly to obtain the favour of the powerful Duke of Buckingham, and for this purpose he helped James's favourite gain the hand of Lady Katherine Manners, then a Roman Catholic, who Williams converted to Anglicanism. Williams had previously held the office of Dean of Salisbury, and he was installed in Westminster Abbey as Dean on 12th July 1620. As mentioned in *A House of Kings*, John Williams was one of the Abbey's greatest benefactors.

At first he spent as much as £4,500 of his own money in restoring the south-east end of the Abbey, and he built a beautiful library out of what was formerly the monks' parlour. It was Williams who repanelled the Jerusalem Chamber at his own expense. It was here that the French Ambassadors were magnificently entertained before the marriage of Charles I and Henrietta Maria. Dean Williams was passionately fond of music, and took immense trouble to organize the services in the Abbey where the organ music was of the sweetest and the singing of the choir very fine. Like Andrewes, Williams was keenly interested in Westminster School.

The Welshman succeeded the disgraced Francis Bacon as Lord Keeper of the Great Seal, though not a lawyer by profession. He was so hardworking that he later mastered much law, being encouraged by Sir Henry Finch, one of the serjeants-at-law. Whilst Williams held the highest legal office in the land, he was also consecrated Bishop of Lincoln in Henry VII's Chapel by the former Dean of Westminster, Mountain, now Bishop of London. Williams got on very well with James. As his biographer Roberts wrote in *Mitre and Musket*: "Their minds chimed well together". Williams was adept in the art of flattery, admiring James's learning, especially his knowledge of Latin. Later Williams fell foul of Charles I and Archbishop Laud.

When the King lay dying at his favourite country mansion, Theobalds, on 24th March 1625, Williams was summoned to his bedside and administered the last rites. James's funeral was on 7th May. A week later Chamberlain wrote to Carleton: "All was performed with great magnificence, but the order was very confused and disorderly." Williams preached the sermon, taking for his text "And Solomon slept with his fathers, and was buried in the City of David his father." Williams eulogized James, eloquently referring to him as "a miracle of Kings and a King of miracles". James was buried in the tomb of his great-great-grandfather, Henry VII, whose daughter Margaret had married James IV of Scotland. How few visitors to the Abbey are aware of this.

Williams, was, however, no longer on friendly terms with the Duke of Buckingham, and the new King had always resented him. Almost immediately Charles I deprived Williams of the Great Seal. To add to his disgrace, he was forbidden to officiate as Dean of Westminster. He was ignominiously instructed to name one of the Abbey prebendaries in his stead. His hated rival William Laud, Bishop of St David's was finally selected.

Consequently Laud performed the same functions at the coronation of Charles I on 2nd February 1626, Candlemas Day, as Andrewes had earlier done at that of his father. Andrewes, as Bishop of Winchester, now merely carried the pater in the coronation procession. For the superstitious, the ceremonial was marred by several sinister omens. For economy or some other reason there was no procession from the Tower. The royal barge balked "Whitehall steps" and was "run aground at the Parliament stairs". Charles I was dressed in white satin instead of the customary purple velvet robe. Perhaps he wanted to reveal "the virgin purity with which he came to be espoused to his Kingdom". The superstitious shuddered, for they remembered him later as being led out as a kind of sacrifice. Many recollected the misfortunes predicted for the 'White King'. Furthermore, the left wing of the dove on the sceptre was broken, and an earth

tremor occurred during the ceremonial. Senhouse, Bishop of
Carlisle preached on the text "I will give thee a crown of life",
which might have been more appropriate for a funeral. It was
extremely tactless of Charles's French Queen, Henrietta Maria,
to refuse to be crowned by non-Catholic bishops and
ostentatiously to absent herself as a spectator from the ceremony.
She merely watched the procession from a window of the
gatehouse at Palace Yard.

Charles himself was a short man, fastidious, reserved, with a
slight impediment in his speech. He was absolutely chaste in his
morals, and after the assassination of the Duke of Buckingham
(whose nickname was 'Steenie') by John Felton in 1628, he fell
very much in love with his vivacious, attractive wife and
succumbed to her influences.

Anxious to honour his friend George Villiers, first Duke of
Buckingham, Charles had him buried in the Chapel of Henry
VII, which had hitherto been mainly reserved for those of royal
descent. The monument was erected by his widow Katherine
(formerly Lady Katherine Manners) and is by Le Sueur. In her
middle age she was to marry Randall Macdonnell, Earl of
Antrim, a handsome Irishman. Also in Buckingham's vault is his
youngest son, Lord Frances Villiers, described by Lord
Clarendon as "a youth of rare beauty and comeliness of person",
killed during the Civil War in a skirmish. Buckingham's parents,
Sir George Villiers of Brokesby in the County of Leicester, and
his second wife Mary Beaumont, are buried in the St Nicholas
Chapel. She was an ambitious, scheming woman, who had given
her favourite son excellent training for the dazzling career which
was his fate. This Villiers monument is a very fine one by the
celebrated sculptor Nicholas Stone, according to Walpole's
Anecdotes. What is curious is the story related by Clarendon of
the appearance of the ghost of Sir George Villiers in his armour
and trunk breeches shortly before the assassination of his son,
before a trembling official of the King's wardrobe, warning him
that unless he altered his conduct and ingratiated himself with the
people, his days were surely numbered.

A much wiser man than Buckingham is interred in St Paul's
Chapel, that Sir Francis Cottingdon (later Lord Cottingdon), a
diplomat and English agent at Madrid, who had in vain tried to

dissuade James I from allowing "Baby Charles" (as his father called him) and Buckingham to go to Spain on their madcap journey to woo the Infanta. One recalls Clarendon's eulogy: "By his natural temper, which was not liable to any transport of anger, or any other passion, but could bear contradiction, and even reproach, without being moved, or put out of his way, for he was very steady in pursuing what he proposed to himself, and had a courage not to be frightened with any opposition..." Cottingdon was to survive Charles I, and to serve him with devotion as Ambassador to Spain. Cottingdon died a Roman Catholic in 1652, and his body was, in 1679 during the later reign of Charles II, brought home from Spain and interred in Westminster Abbey. The upper part of the tomb was erected to the memory of his wife, who predeceased him, and is by Le Sueur. According to the State Papers (Charles I) 18th July 1634, the sculptor Hubert Le Sueur of the parish of great St Bartholomew was commissioned to do the work for £400. Lord Cottingdon's monument is very beautiful and austere, composed of black and white marble by the one-eyed sculptor Fanelli. The Abbey is rich in elaborate monuments of personalities of the Stuart age. Among them Lionel Cranfield, Earl of Middlesex (interred there in 1645), who, owing to his remarkable financial ability, rose from the humble position of a London apprentice to become Lord Treasurer of England during the reign of James I. Nor must be omitted the enormous and not altogether pleasing monument to the memory of a great nobleman and cousin of James I, Ludovic Stuart, Duke of Richmond and Lennox, buried in the south of the central aisle of Henry VII's Chapel. He had been James VI's (as he was then) companion to Gowrie House, near Perth when an attempt was made on the King's life. After his death, his widow requested Charles I to order that the stone partition should be removed and that an iron gate should be placed there instead. A famous poet to be buried in the north aisle of the nave was Ben Jonson, who died in 1637. Like Edmund Spenser "the Prince of Poets in his tyme", who lies in Poets' Corner. Jonson died in dire poverty. He had intimate associations with Westminster, having been educated at Westminster School under Camden, and spending two hours a week studying music under the choirmaster. His last years were spent near to the Abbey, in a house that formerly stood between it and St Margaret's Church. There is a tradition that Jonson was jesting one day with Dean Williams about being buried with the other poets and said that he could not afford the honour, "No Sir, six feet long by two feet wide is too much for me; two feet by two feet will do." He may have also asked Charles I to grant him a favour; "What is it?" asked the King, "Give me eighteeen inches of square ground." "Where?" asked Charles, "In Westminster Abbey." Perhaps this is the origin of the story that he was buried standing upright. John Aubrey relates that King Charles sent Ben Jonson £10 when he was dying.

It is related in *A House of Kings* how Archbishop Laud managed to obtain Dean Williams's condemnation in the Star Chamber on a Treason Charge. It is almost miraculous how Williams stubbornly held on to his Deanery though his enemies tried to make him surrender it. During 1637 Williams was imprisoned in the Tower and fined £10,000. The years which followed, when the bitter struggle between King and Parliament became more acute, culminating in the Civil War, were sad years in the history of the Abbey. Fighting broke out in the cloisters of the Abbey between rival groups. Consequently the sub-dean and prebendaries were forced to order that the gates of the close should be locked at 10 p.m. Williams, for some time released from the Tower, was appointed Archbishop of York in November 1641, and he retained his Deanery at Westminster for three more years. There were serious riots at Westminster when a vociferous host of apprentices surged about the Abbey shouting, "No bishop, no King!" Fortunately the Abbey staff together with the Westminster School boys resisted the worst excesses of the mob. Attempts were made to pull down the organs and destroy the altar. At this desperate juncture, Williams, strongly supported by his servants, and others defended the Abbey and managed to save the regalia, for which he was coolly complimented by King Charles.

The brave little Welshman, Dean Williams, a great patron of the Abbey, died on 25th March 1650, more than a year after Charles I had been executed in Whitehall. Williams is buried in Llandegary Church, near Radnor in Caernarvonshire, the county of his birth, not in Westminster Abbey.

For some months during 1642, the Chapter under Robert Newell, the Subdean, carried on the Abbey services, but a parliamentary committee, under the chairmanship of Sir Robert Harley of Brampton Bryan, Herefordshire, ordered that various monuments of superstition and idolatry should be abolished in the Abbey Church. Torrigiano's high altar in Henry VII's Chapel was taken down, and the painted images of another altar despoiled. Harley, a confirmed anti-papist, had been equally zealous in stripping Leominster Church of a crucifix and a window of stained glass. Dean Stanley, in his *Memorial of Westminster Abbey*, is strangely silent about the acts of vandalism. He fails to describe the conduct of the coarse soldiers stationed in the Abbey during the summer of 1643. How they smashed the organ to bits and pawned its pipes "at several ale-houses for pots of ale".

Throughout these tumultuous years and the vicissitudes which the Abbey was compelled to suffer, it endured as the burial place for sovereigns, illustrious Parliamentarians and admirals of vast renown. It is greater in spirit than the people, who cast their shadowy, fleeting influence upon the place and then are gone for ever.

James Howell, writing during the Commonwealth period in *Londinopolis* (published in 1657) mentions: "Now the Abbey of Westminster hath bin always held the greatest sanctuary, a rendezvous of devotion of the whole iland: whereunto the situation of the very place seemes to contribute much, and to strike a holy kind of reverence and sweetness of melting piety into the hearts of the beholders." How true today, despite the great crowds thronging its pavements.

After the trial of Charles I in Westminster Hall in January 1649, followed by his execution, the House of Commons decided that Charles Stuart should be buried at St George's Chapel, Windsor. It was argued that Westminster Abbey was both too famous a place and too accessible for their purpose. The Duke of Richmond was charged with the duty of arranging the burial at a total cost of five hundred pounds. When the royal coffin was carried out of St George's Hall, thick flakes of snow began to fall, so that the black velvet pall now became white. "So went our white King to his grave!" remarked his devoted servants in tears, recalling perhaps their King dressed in white at his coronation.

Oliver Cromwell was solemnly installed as Lord Protector of the Kingdom on Friday, 26th June 1657 in Westminster Hall. For this State occasion the coronation chair was brought out of the Abbey. Indeed certain aspects of the service resembled previous coronation services for Kings of England. It was the Speaker of the House of Commons who invested the Lord Protector with his purple ermine-trimmed robe, and the *Mercurius Politicus*, a journal published during the Commonwealth period, later reported, "The habit anciently used at the solemn investiture of princes." Antonia Fraser mentions in her *Cromwell Our Chief of Men*, that the Speaker girded him with his sword and handed him his sceptre. Only the crown was not set on the dictator's head. The office of Lord Protector was not hereditary, but Cromwell had power to choose his own successor. Ambassadors, aldermen of the City, members of Parliament and judges, were present at this historic event.

The first Parliament of the Protectorate met on 3rd September 1654, an auspicious day for the superstitious Cromwell, for it was the anniversary of his two great victories of Dunbar and Worcester. Now there was only a short address followed by a sermon in Westminster Abbey. During 1657 there was an attempt by some discontented secret agents, whose head was Miles Sindercombe, to murder Cromwell as he left Westminster Abbey. During the service there was a sermon by Oliver Cromwell's chaplain, John Owen. The conspirators had hatched their conspiracy in a house in King Street, Westminster. The plot miscarried because Cromwell was surrounded by large numbers of men.

This was an unsettled, unhappy period in the Abbey's history. A corporal and nine soldiers were stationed in Westminster Abbey on Sundays to keep order. Preachers, especially those with marked papist sympathies, were subjected to heckling and constant interruption.

The famous headmaster of Westminster School, Dr Richard Busby, was opposed to Puritan rule, but felt it politic to allow his pupils to attend the services of the Presbyterian clergymen at the Abbey. However, he had strong royalist sympathies and took the initiative in making his boys pray for Charles I on the day of his execution, 30th January. When we pass the tablet which records his death during William III's reign, for he lived to a great age and was buried beneath the black-and-white pavement, we think of the affection this man inspired in his pupils.

Dean Stanley, in his *Historical Memorials of Westminster Abbey*, considers that the monuments in the Abbey, which suffered so horribly during the reign of Henry VIII, remained uninjured under Cromwell. Antonia Fraser, in her recent biography of Cromwell, supports Stanley in his view. Surely, however, it is only partly true. Earlier in 1643, at least, Cromwell's soldiers inflicted damage on some of the Abbey's medieval tombs, such as the tomb of Aymer de Valence, Earl of Pembroke near the high altar. In their ignorance they broke stained-glass windows, and robbed the Abbey of gold and silver ornaments. Besides his more humane qualities and his strong family sense, his biographer mentions "his manic rage which drove him into battle, which caused him to have cut down the Irish priests without regret, and have the King killed and feel not the slightest tremor afterwards". Such a man is either loved for some great qualities or hated by many for his ruthlessness and savagery.

When Cromwell's able friend and son-in-law, Henry Ireton died in Ireland in 1650-1651, his body was brought back from Limerick and lay in state in Somerset House. There was a magnificent funeral in Westminster Abbey, and Oliver himself was chief mourner. John Evelyn watched it, deeply impressed as Cromwell's "mock parliament-men, officers and 40 poore men in gownes" filed past on the way to the Abbey. John Owen preached the funeral sermon, taking his text from Daniel and praising "the stout rebel", as Evelyn described him, for his spiritual and civil wisdom. His body was later disinterred.

Admiral Robert Blake, a great seaman of the Cromwellian era, who fought so heroically against the Spaniards, died in 1657, and he was buried "amongst the Kings with all the solemnity possible" in Henry VII's Chapel. There is a report among the Domestic State Papers from the Admiralty Commissioners that Blake's interment cost £550.

Oliver Cromwell, too, gave his mother Elizabeth Cromwell, to whom he was devoted, a grand funeral in the Abbey when she died at a very advanced age. Hundreds of flickering torches enhanced its austere beauty. Cromwell was deeply attached to his favourite daughter Elizabeth (Bettie) Claypole, who died in 1658. Her body was borne by barge on an August evening from Hampton Court to Westminster. It was not until after midnight that the last funeral rites were performed in the Henry VII Chapel. Bettie Claypole was the only one of her family whose body was not disturbed after the Restoration. Diligent search was made for her resting-place, but it could not be discovered until 1725, when workmen making some alterations in the Chapel for the installations of the Knights of the Bath stumbled upon it. Dean Stanley discusses the matter in his book, and it is also referred to by Antonia Fraser.

The longing, almost an obsession, among distinguished persons to be buried in Westminster Abbey reached its height during the Commonwealth, if not earlier. Among those to be buried in St John the Baptist's Chapel were Robert Devereux, third Earl of Essex, son of that ill-fated favourite of Elizabeth I, who had been executed in 1601. Essex is chiefly renowned as the general-in-chief of the Parliamentary army. He died in 1646, but on the night of his funeral some ruffians entered the Abbey, broke the head of his effigy, and slit the buff coat which he had worn at Edgehill, and other damage. It is hard to understand the mentality of people prepared to act in such a wanton fashion, whatever one's political sympathies. Another important Parliamentary personality – John Pym, 'King Pym' as he was nicknamed by the Royalists, was given a magnificent funeral when he died in 1643. In the presence of many members of the House of Commons and Lords he was interred at the entrance of the Chapel of St John the Baptist. Eighteen years later Pym's body was disinterred, and flung, together with other Parliamentarians, into a pit outside the Abbey walls.

John Evelyn was an eyewitness at Oliver Cromwell's funeral on 23rd November 1658 in Westminster Abbey. "The Joyfullest funeral that I ever saw," he wrote; "for there was none that cried but dogs, which the soldiers hooted away with a barborous noise, drinking and taking tobacco in the streetes as they went." Evelyn, a staunch Anglican, was always hostile to Oliver Cromwell. The body of the Protector lay in state in Somerset House, and the streets were lined with soldiers as the hearse proceeded on its way to the Abbey. Many exulted at his death –

curiously enough on 3rd September, a day formerly of triumph for him. The extravagance of the display made it seem that a prince of royal blood was being buried rather than a dictator. Abraham Cowley the poet, later to be buried in the Abbey, and a Royalist, found the high cost of the funeral distasteful. It is said to have cost £28,000 or more. What was called "Oliver Cromwell's Vault" was prepared at the east end of Henry VII's Chapel. After the Restoration, the bodies of Cromwell, Ireton and Bradshaw, who had presided at the trial of Charles I were disinterred. On 1st February 1661 the three headless corpses were taken to Tyburn, and buried under the gallows, their faces turned towards Whitehall, a grisly sight for the mob, teaching them the folly and savage fate reserved for traitors.

The coronation of Charles II on St George's Day, 23rd April 1661 was a far more joyous ceremony that those of earlier or later Stuart sovereigns. Four days before, sixty-eight Knights of the Bath had been created after a bathing ceremony in the Painted Chamber at Westminster of deep significance because it was the last occasion when this ceremony occurred in connection with a coronation. On 22nd April the procession from the Tower to Whitehall was revived where Charles II created Edward Hyde the first Earl of Clarendon, and other peers. Both Pepys and Evelyn described it, but Pepys's well-known account is more entertaining. "About four I rose and got to the Abbey," he wrote, "and with much ado, by the favour of Mr Cooper, his man, did get up into a great scaffold accross the north end of the Abbey, where with a great deal of patience I sat from past four till eleven before the King came in. And a great pleasure it was to see the Abbey raised in the middle, all covered with red ... All the officers, even the very fiddlers, in red vests ..." The Dean of Westminster, who officiated, was Dr John Earle, the King's Chaplain, and friend whilst in exile. Gilbert Sheldon, Bishop of London, presented the King to the people, who cried out "God save King Charles II." The sermon was preached by Morley, Bishop of Worcester. Dr Richard Busby carried the ampulla, while Archbishop Juxon, now old and infirm, anointed and crowned the King. The customary coronation feast was held in Westminster Hall, and Sir Edward Dymoke, as Lord of the

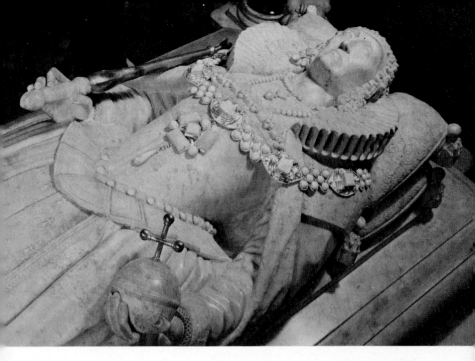

The tomb effigy of Elizabeth I by Maximilian Colt and John de Critz

The tomb effigy of Mary Queen of Scots by William and Cornelius Cure

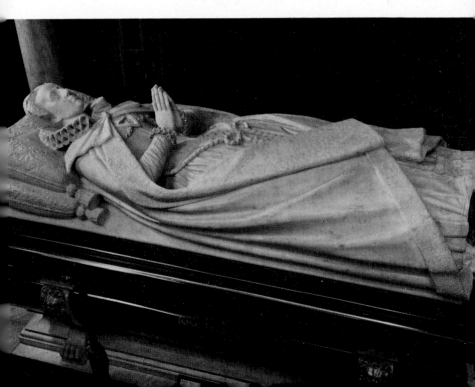

The monument to Gabriel Goodman, Dean of Westminster

Manor of Scrivelsby in Lincolnshire, appeared as the King's Champion.

It was only on his death-bed that Charles II was admitted into the Roman Catholic Church. He was a natural sceptic, and could hardly be described as a religious man. Charles was in the habit of falling asleep at sermons. On one occasion one of his chaplains interrupted his sermon to remark to the Duke of Lauderdale, "My Lord, My Lord! You snore so loud you will wake the King!", which richly amused Charles.

John Evelyn was much attached to the new Dean of Westminster, Dr John Earle. He described him as "a most humble, meeke, but chereful man, an excellent scholar, and rare preacher". Evelyn was a guest at Earle's consecration as Bishop of Worcester and mentions the magnificent dinner afterwards, which cost nearly £600.

Once again Westminster Abbey became the last resting-place for princes and princesses of the House of Stuart. The festivities at Whitehall were marred by the death of Charles's younger brother Henry of Oatlands, Duke of Gloucester, who died during September 1660. Whilst in exile abroad his mother, Queen Henrietta Maria, had in vain tried to convert him to Roman Catholicism and to make him enter the Jesuits' College, but the boy had stubbornly refused. "I will see your face no more," his mother had harshly told him. Pepys relates that Gloucester died of smallpox owing to the great negligence of the doctors. His body was borne down Somerset House stairs, and taken by water to be buried in the same vault as Mary Queen of Scots and Arbella Stuart in Westminster Abbey. Clarendon warmly praised him: "The finest youth of the most manly understanding that I have ever known", while Sir John Reresby considered that he was far from insensible to female charms. Elizabeth of Bohemia, Charles II's aunt, "A princess resplendent in darkness", as Sir Henry Wotton beautifully described her, after a stormy life full of vicissitudes, passed her last years in London. Evelyn relates that on the night of her burial in Westminster Abbey and the following day there "fell such a storm of hail, thunder and lightening as never was seene the like in any men's memorie ..."

How unfortunate the Stuarts were, for during the very year of her brother's triumph, Mary of Orange (mother of the future William III) died of smallpox. She was buried in the Abbey on 29th December 1660, near the Duke of Gloucester. Preaching on Christmas Day, the Dean of Westminster, Dr Earle, alluded to the public sorrow. Among the prelates buried was Brian Duppa, Bishop of Winchester, and in the State Papers was the order arranged for the procession for Duppa, "Prelate of the Order of the Garter from the Strand to Westminster Abbey."

John Dolben succeeded Dr Earle as Dean of Westminster and was installed on 31st December 1661. He had been a Westminster Schoolboy when Dr Richard Busby was headmaster, and he had served Charles I during the Civil War, being wounded at Marston Moor and the Siege of York. It was during this period, for Dolben's tenure as Dean lasted twenty years, that the see of Rochester was united with the Deanery, thus benefiting this impoverished bishopric financially and providing a town residence. Pepys visited Dolben during 1667, at his lodgings in the Abbey to see an organ. "He lives like a great prelate", he wrote, "his lodgings being very good", but he was then in disgrace at Court. While Dolben was Dean many repairs were made to the fabric of the Abbey. On one occasion when Pepys was attending a service in the Abbey during 1660, some plaster had fallen on him filling him with fear. Widmore describes Dolben as "an extraordinarily lovely person, though grown too fat; of an open countenance, a lively piercing eye, and a majestic presence ..."

According to Clarendon, during the Great Fire of London in 1666, Charles II was more afraid for the Abbey than for his own Palace of Whitehall. Taswell, a Westminster schoolboy described the Great Fire "when the flakes at last reached Westminster". The Dean was quietly efficient in organizing the pupils of Westminster School to fetch water from St Dunstan's in the east "where we happily extinguished the fire". On the night that fire blazed over St Paul's it was so bright that Taswell could read his book very clearly.

Charles II is said to have gently chided Dolben for sticking too close to his manuscript when preaching, but his contemporaries considered him an eloquent preacher. Several famous people were buried in Westminster Abbey when Dolben was Dean, among them Abraham Cowley, whose funeral during August 1667 was described by Evelyn: "From Wallingford House his body was conveyed to Westminster Abbey in a hearse with six horses and all funeral decency, neare a hundred coaches of noblemen and persons of qualitie following, among these all the witts of the towne." He lies next to Geoffrey Chaucer and near Edmund Spenser. Also interred here are the poet Sir John Denham, Thomas Killigrew the witty manager of the King's Theatre, and a boon companion of Charles II, and Sir William Davenant, one-time Poet Laureate and manager of the Duke's Theatre.

George Monck, first Duke of Albemarle, chiefly remembered today for his vital role in restoring Charles II to his kingdom, was given a grand funeral in the north aisle of Henry VII's Chapel. Andrew Marvell wrote: "It is almost three months, on 21st March (Monck died on 3rd January 1679) and he yet lies in the dark unburied, and no talk of him." Charles II bore the cost of the funeral himself, and Dolben officiated as Dean. Francis Sandford, the Lancaster Herald, who wrote a detailed account of the ceremony, mentions Ensign John Churchill (later the great Duke of Marlborough) on duty. He was not quite twenty.

A greater man than George Monck was buried in Westminster Abbey in January 1674. This was Edward Hyde, Earl of Clarendon, who had served Charles II so faithfully as a statesman. However, he was compelled to spend the last few years of his life in exile, described by a traveller at Rouen as a "fair, ruddy, fat, middle-statured handsome man". He suffered from gout and found consolation in writing *The History of the Great Rebellion*, and other literary work. He died at Rouen. His reputation as a historian remains very high. He is buried below the steps leading from the Henry VII Chapel. Many of his family, including his sons Henry (second Earl of Clarendon), and Laurence, (created Earl of Rochester) are interred there. Anne Hyde, Duchess of York is buried in the south aisle of Henry VII's Chapel. In the centre of the choir is an inscription commemorating Edward Hyde's niece, Dame Ann Carey (*née* Hyde).

Thomas Sprat succeeded John Dolben as Dean of Westminster in 1683, since Dolben had been appointed Archbishop of York. Sprat also became Bishop of Rochester. The new Dean was not a

man of very strong religious principles, being perhaps too supine
in his attitude to various monarchs. He was, however, devoted to
literature and possessed a great admiration for John Dryden. He
was indeed one of the chief precursors of the Augustan Age of
English prose.

Charles II, who concealed his remarkable ability as a King
under an assumed air of indolence and nonchalance, died on 6th
February 1685. Few kings have been more mourned by their
subjects for he was much beloved. The new King, James II,
wanted his brother to be buried privately at night, and was
opposed to Charles being publicly subjected to Anglican rites,
especially as he had been partly responsible for his brother's
conversion to Roman Catholicism on his death bed. Prince
George of Denmark was chief mourner and the merry monarch
was interred in the southern aisle of Henry VII's Chapel.

James II was a Roman Catholic convert, a man of very strong
religious conviction married to a papist Queen Mary of Modena,
an Italian, who was very jealous of her husband and absolutely
devoted to him. Their joint coronation took place on St George's
Day, 23rd April. James's instructions that the traditional
procession from the Tower to the Abbey should be cancelled for
reasons of economy, was an error, for the crowd loved it. The
King and Queen, a woman of striking Italianate beauty, were
privately anointed in St James's Palace the night before the
Westminster Abbey ceremony by Father Mansuete, a Franciscan.
William Sancroft, Archbishop of Canterbury, had been
instructed by James that their majesties would not receive the
sacraments, but that the Anglican rites should be used during the
service.

Francis Sandford's description of James's coronation is a
fascinating, detailed account. Nowhere do we get a better idea of
the important functions of the Deans of Westminster. Early in
the morning it was the duty of Dr Sprat with the assistance of the
prebendaries to consecrate the holy oil for their majesties'
anointing, and to give order for bringing the regalia in solemn
procession to Westminster Hall. Dr Sprat was dressed in a
surplice and rich cope of purple velvet, embroidered with gold
and silver. During the ceremony St Edward's Crown on a
cushion of cloth of gold was borne by the Dean.

Francis Sandford describes James, then aged fifty-three, "in his royal robes of crimson velvet, furred with ermine, and bordered with gold lace", and his Queen, so dignified and majestic, superb, like her namesake Queen Mary nearer our own time, consort of George V. She wore "purple velvet, richly furred with ermine and bordered with gold lace, with a circle of gold on Her Majesties head, under a canopy of cloth of gold". One curious ancient custom was revived, the post of hereditary herb-woman and Mary Dowle was assisted by six women each carrying "nine baskets full of sweet herbs and flowers".

As the Queen entered the choir, forty scholars of Westminster School cried "*Vivat Regina Maria*", and as the King ascended the theatre they greeted him in the same manner, "*Vivat Jacobus Rex*". Francis Turner, Bishop of Ely preached the sermon, taking his text from the First Book of Chronicles, "Then Solomon sat on the throne of the Lord as King, instead of David his father, and prospered, and all Israel obeyed him."

During the anointing ceremony, four Knights of the Garter, James Butler, Duke of Ormonde, Christopher, Duke of Albemarle, the Duke of Beaufort, and the Earl of Mulgrave, held a pall of cloth of gold over the King. Dean Sprat brought the ampulla and oil from the altar, and Archbishop Sancroft poured the holy oil into the spoon, and proceeded to anoint the King in the form of a cross. For the investing, the Dean put the buskins and sandals of cloth of gold on the King's feet, and brought the spurs from the altar to be delivered to the Lord Great Chamberlain, among other duties. Then at exactly three o'clock, Archbishop Sancroft, benign and mild-tempered, assisted by Dean Sprat, and various bishops, set the crown on James's head. Unfortunately the crown was too large, and it descended over the upper part of the King's face, which the Queen considered an evil omen. Henry Sidney, who disliked James, tried to steady it, remarking to the King "that it was not the first time a Sidney had supported the Crown". Again, owing to the clumsiness of the Barons of the Cinque Ports, the canopy fell over the King. The behaviour of Mary of Modena was more dignified throughout the service than the King's. "I never saw greater devotion on any countenance," remarked the Dean of Peterborough.

Dean Sprat found himself in an embarrassing position owing to

James's arbitrary policy as King. He was an Anglican High Churchman, and agreed to serve on the Ecclesiastical Commission set up by James in 1686 to try Henry Compton, Bishop of London for refusing, though commanded by the King, to inhibit John Sharp, Vicar of St Giles-in-the-Field. However, he withdrew from the Commission when Compton was suspended.

By the Declaration of Indulgence, liberty was given to Roman Catholics and Dissenters to worship as they wanted, although not enacted by Parliament. Westminster Abbey was one of the few churches where the Declaration was read, whether by Dean Sprat or by one of the minor canons is of little importance. The second Lord Dartmouth, son of James II's staunch friend George Legge, the first Earl, was then a boy at Westminster School, and heard it read in the Abbey, though the bulk of the congregation showed their hostility by their loud murmurs and interruptions. Evelyn wrote: "I hear the Declaration was read in the Abbey Church, Westminster, but almost universally forborne throughout all London." These were dramatic times for England, reflected in the Abbey's history. Many rejoiced at the acquittal of the seven Bishops in 1688, and the Abbey bells pealed merrily, but Dean Sprat ordered them to be silenced.

The most important funeral during James II's short reign, was that of James Butler, first Duke of Ormonde, a great man, who had given devoted services to Charles I and Charles II as Lord Lieutenant in Ireland. It was fortunate for him that he did not live to see King James forced into exile. Ormonde and his family were interred in the Henry VII Chapel. It is a matter of reproach that the Duke of Ormonde was not given a public memorial, nor has one been raised since his death.

Whether or not Dean Sprat was pusillanimous in his relations with James II, there were among the prebendaries men like Symon Patrick, later Bishop of Chichester, who favoured the party of the King's son-in-law, Prince William of Orange. He lived in a newly built house in the Little Cloister, that lovely part of the Abbey where one can hear the murmur of the fountain. He was a close friend of Thomas Tenison, then Vicar of St Martins-in-the-Fields, later Archbiship of Canterbury. Patrick and Tenison were together on the night of 7th August 1688, when Tenison told his friend in confidence that William of Orange intended to come over to England with an army. He would be wise to carry his valuables out of London. On a foul night of storm and rain, 17th December – the same day on which the Prince of Orange had arrived at St James's Palace, there was a loud knock at the door. It was the Bishop of St Asaph who told the two clergymen that he was charged by the bishops to wait upon the Prince to ascertain his pleasure when they might all pay their duty to him.

Another of the prebendaries, Robert South, who had a reputation for his brilliant sermons, once preached before Charles II, who on this occasion at least was not asleep. He alluded to "such a bankrupt, beggarly fellow as Cromwell entering the Parliament House with a threadbare torn cloak and a greasy hat, and perhaps neither of them paid for". As related by Dean Stanley, the King roared with laughter and turning to Laurence Hyde, Earl of Rochester, remarked, "Ods fish, Lory, your Chaplain must be a bishop, therefore put me in mind of him at the next death." South, however, was offered the Deanery on Sprat's death in 1713, but refused it on the grounds of age.

King James and Queen Mary of Modena fled the country to take refuge at Louis XIV's Court. Four months later, King William III and Queen Mary II were jointly crowned in Westminster Abbey on 11th April 1689. The Archbishop of Canterbury, William Sancroft a man of high honour, refused to take part in the ceremony because of his former oath of allegiance to James II, and some of the bishops were also absent. The militant Henry Compton, Bishop of London was chosen in his place to crown the King and Queen.

The new Queen, tall and graceful, had hardly completed her toilet when she heard of her father, James II's landing in Ireland. This may well have caused a delay to the start of this joyless coronation. Planned to begin at eleven o'clock, it finally began at half-past one. There was no procession from the Tower of London to Westminster. Neither the Bishops of Durham or Bath and Wells who normally took a prominent part in the ceremony, were present. Some of the peers, including the Queen's uncle Lord Clarendon, ostentatiously absented themselves.

One of Sprat's duties as Bishop of Rochester and Dean of

Westminster, was to advise William how to conduct himself during the service. Unfortunately there were hitches. William who was feeling ill, failed to respond when asked to make the customary offerings, a roll of silk and thirty pieces of silver. There was an awkward silence until Lord Danby lent him the required sum. Somebody erred in setting the diamond and ruby ring, which William had given Mary, on his finger instead of hers. For Mary this was naturally an anxious day, and she wrote of it: "The coronation came on; that was to be all vanity." Mary sat in a special coronation chair, which had to be made for her, which is now in the Abbey museum. As Mary was lifted into the chair, her sister Princess Anne said, a little pertly, "Madam, I pity your fatigue." Whereupon the Queen snubbed her with the retort, "A crown, Sister, is not so heavy as it seems." It was Dr Lloyd, Bishop of St Asaph, who presented the King and Queen to the people, and Bishop Burnet, a great admirer of the new Queen, received great applause for his sermon, according to Evelyn.

The coronation banquet was in Westminster Hall, but the King's Champion, Sir Charles Dymoke (son of James II's Champion) was very tardy in putting in an appearance. A tradition exists, as mentioned by Agnes Strickland, that as the Champion flung down his gauntlet, an old woman upon crutches hobbled out of the crowd took it up, leaving a lady's glove in its place, and presumably her gesture was intended to answer the challenge. Lamberty, a contemporary writer, merely records: "I heard the sound of his gauntlet when he flung it on the ground, but as the light in Westminster Hall had utterly failed, no person could distinguish what was done."

Westminster Abbey is proud of her great son, Henry Purcell, a musician of genius, appointed organist in 1679 when Charles II was on the throne. It is, perhaps, insufficiently realized that the Merry Monarch was an eager patron of musicians and they surely missed him when he died. Purcell's elegy "If Pray're and Tears" commemorated Charles. His intimate association with Westminster Abbey influenced his work, and it pulsates with feeling for his native England. Whether Purcell was born in Westminster is not absolutely certain, but after his marriage the musician lived in St Anne's Lane, Old Pie Street, and was almost certainly born there. Purcell died in November 1695, and was given a grand funeral in the Abbey. He has been described as "The Chaucer" of the musicians' corner in the north transept. Some who attended the sad event must have had vivid recollections ten years before of the choir going before James II and Mary of Modena as they entered the Abbey for their coronation, and the beauty of Purcell's anthem "I Was Glad When They Said", flooding the building with celestial light. How privileged they were, too, to hear his most glorious work heard at the coronation, "My Heart is Inditing." It was Lady Elizabeth Howard, John Dryden's wife, Purcell's friend and former pupil, who wrote his epitaph: "Here lyes Henry Purcell, Esqr. who left this Life, and is gone to that Blessed Place where only his Harmony can be exceeded."

Almost a year earlier died Queen Mary II, aged only thirty-two. The Jacobite Earl of Ailesbury referred to her as "this incomparable princess", and Burnet praised her for her virtue and understanding, but there was a core of hardness in her character, partly explicable when we consider her difficult life with William. Her funeral in Westminster Abbey, took place on 5th March 1695, a raw icy winter day. Members of Parliament and four hundred poor women walked in the procession in black cloaks. All the nobility attended, the mayor, aldermen and judges. As the procession moved on, sixty cannons resounded in St James's Park and the Tower. In the Abbey a boy's voice singing Purcell's elegy "O Dive Custos Aurice Domus, Maria, Maria" could be heard.

George Savile, Marquis of Halifax, a remarkable statesman, who served three kings, and nicknamed "The Trimmer", was interred in the north aisle in Queen Elizabeth's Chapel. He died in 1695, and today we remember him for his perceptive character study of Charles II and for his wit, which delighted that amiable monarch. Also for his speech on James II's behalf at the time of the Exclusion Crisis, though James disliked him.

During 1692 — a year which buzzed with rumours of Jacobite plots against William III — Thomas Sprat, Dean of Westminster, Bishop of Rochester, was suspected of complicity and put under house arrest, among other prominent people, including the Earl of Marlborough imprisoned in the Tower. The evidence incriminating Sprat was concealed in a flower plot in the Bishop's garden, but it was almost certainly concocted by a perjured villain named Robert Young and untrue. However, Sprat was not well disposed towards William II. When John Dryden died in May 1700, Dean Sprat was eager to officiate at the poet-dramatist's funeral, though Dryden was now a Roman Catholic convert. Dryden died in poverty in Gerrard Street, Soho, and was given a grand burial in Poets' Corner. So, Dryden is honoured today as one of the greatest satirical poets.

William III, a consummate statesman, but not a great soldier, was also interred in Westminster Abbey. He was buried privately on the night of 12th April 1702, in his wife's vault in Henry VII's Chapel. Prince George of Denmark, who had so often been the butt of William's moroseness, was the chief mourner.

William had been fond of Princess Anne's only surviving son, William, Duke of Gloucester, who died in 1700. This promising boy of eleven, who would have ascended the throne after his mother if he had lived, had as his governor the Earl of Marlborough. His coffin was borne to Henry VII's Chapel, where he was interred.

Anne, the last Stuart Queen, who succeeded her brother-in-law, was crowned on St George's Day 1702. She was the only monarch who had to be carried in her sedan chair to her coronation from St James's Palace to the Abbey, owing to an acute attack of gout, a humiliating blow to her pride. Sarah, Countess of Marlborough, the Queen's Groom of the Stole and Mistress of the Robes, saw to it that Anne was finely dressed in crimson velvet with an under-robe of gold tissue. Sarah's accounts reveal that it cost £10. 15s. for "dressing Her Majesty's head", and it was found necessary to supply "a head of hair with long locks and puffs costing £12.". Anne enjoyed great popularity, and along the Broad Sanctuary the windows and balconies were crowded with the jubilant people rejoicing that 'Dutch William' had been succeeded by their English Queen. Her husband, fat and portly, dressed in a resplendent blue and silver uniform, as Generalissimo, walked before the Queen.

Archbishop Tenison crowned Queen Anne, while Sharp, Archbishop of York preached the sermon using the text: "Kings Shall Be Thy Nursing Fathers and Queens Thy Nursing

Mothers." Anne was a conventional Protestant, and hers was a comfortable, practical religion, no doubt giving her consolation when she was overwhelmed by sorrow and helping her to do her duty. Sarah, Duchess of Marlborough, dressed in black, is said to have haunted the cloisters of Westminster Abbey after her son, Lord Blandford died at Cambridge in 1703.

There were perhaps no elements of greatness in the character of Queen Anne, a woman of meagre intelligence, but she had at least an understanding of the people whom she ruled and an innate sense of what was best for them.

Thomas Sprat, Dean of Westminster and Bishop of Rochester, died on 20th May 1713, and was succeeded by Francis Atterbury, who had been a scholar at Westminster School, a man of very strong personality, though somewhat cantankerous and quarrelsome.

Queen Anne died in Kensington House on 1st August 1714, and was interred in the vault beside Prince George of Denmark, and her sister Queen Mary. Dean Stanley tells us "that her unwieldy frame filled a coffin larger even than her gigantic spouse".

BIBLIOGRAPHY

Aikin, Lucy, *Memoirs of the Court of James I* (1822)

Akrigg, G.P.V., *Jacobean Pageant* (1962)

Chute, Marchette, *Ben Jonson of Westminster*

Earle, Peter, *The Life and Times of James II* (1972)

Memoirs and Correspondence of John Evelyn (1827)

Falkus, Christopher, *The Life and Times of Charles II* (1972)

Fraser, Lady Antonia, *Cromwell Our Chief of Men* (1973)

Handover, P.M., *Arbella Stuart* (1957)

Diary and Correspondence of Samuel Pepys (Ed. Richard, Lord Braybrooke 4 Vols. (1894)

Roberts, B., *Mitre and Musket* (1938)

Sandford, Francis, *The History of the Coronation of the Most High, most Mighty and most Excellent Monarch James II* (London 1687)

Sandford, Francis, *The Order and Ceremonies used for the Internment of George Duke of Albemarle* (folio 1670)

Stanley, Arthur Penrhyn, *Historical Memorials of Westminster*
Strickland, Agnes, *Lives of the Queens of England* Vol. VII
Turner, F.C., *James II* (1948)
Watson, D.R., *The Life and Times of Charles I* (1972)
Williams, Ethel Carleton, *Anne of Denmark* (1970)
Zimmerman, Franklin B., *Henry Purcell 1659-1695. His Life and Times* (1967)

8

Hanoverian Sovereigns and Edward VII

George Lewis, son of the Elector of Hanover Ernest Augustus and of Sophia, the clever grand-daughter of James I of England, was not an agreeable personality. He was coarse, vindictive, slow-witted, unimaginative and was on the whole uncultured. "I hate all boets and bainters," he once said and they reciprocated his sentiments. Yet, like most Germans, he had a genuine appreciation of music, and his patronage of George Frideric Handel was of inestimable benefit to English music.

It was George Lewis Elector of Hanover, who at the age of fifty-four, succeeded Queen Anne on the throne as George I. The new King spoke no English, though conversant with French, and when he was crowned in Westminster Abbey on 20th October 1714 by the Archbishop of Canterbury, much of the ceremony was completely incomprehensible to him. George disliked pageantry and splendour, and he cannot have felt at ease in his royal robes of crimson velvet. The Bishop of Oxford preached the sermon, and especially mentioned the eight glorious campaigns under the wise conduct of the Duke of Marlborough, now returned to England from exile and enjoying the King's favour.

Mary, Countess Cowper, relates an entertaining story in her diary concerning the former Catherine Sedley, a former mistress of James II, now Lady Portmore, a witty, but coarse woman. "She stood underneath me," she wrote, "and when the Archbishop went round the throne demanding the consent of the people, she turned about to me, and said, 'Does the old fool think that anybody here will say no to his question when there are so many drawn swords?' " During the service, Lady Portmore noticed two other familiar faces in the congregation, Louise de Kéroualle, Duchess of Portsmouth (a former mistress of Charles II) and Elizabeth Villiers, Lady Orkney (a former mistress of William III), so made the delicious remark: "Good God! Who would have thought we three whores would have met together here."

When Henry St John Viscount Bolingbroke, an unprincipled but brilliant politician, bowed three times as he made his servile homage, George I inquired his name and looked coldly past him. Bolingbroke had opposed the Hanoverians, and was almost immediately to flee to France where he attached himself to 'James III' the Pretender, whose cause he was later to betray.

Francis Atterbury as Dean of Westminster, played his part admirably at George's coronation, though not well disposed towards the King. His functions were all the more complicated by George's lack of awareness and understanding of the religious significance. There is a strong tradition that Atterbury, also Bishop of Rochester, a high churchman sympathetic to 'James III', "The King over the water", wanted to proclaim him, in his bishop's lawn sleeves at Charing Cross as his half-sister, Queen Anne, lay dying. He was deeply attached to Westminster Abbey. Visitors who gaze today with delight at the beauty of the rose window in the north transept, are seldom aware that this turbulent but great Dean was responsible for selecting the subjects for the window. He superintended the work on the repair and restoration of the north front by Sir Christopher Wren, at that period surveyor of the Abbey. Atterbury was naturally keenly interested in Westminster School, and was responsible for taking the initiative in advocating the rebuilding of the new dormitory in the College Garden. Like Andrewes, he was an eloquent and outspoken preacher, and delighted in the society of poets and writers such as Alexander Pope and Joseph Addison.

Handel identified himself completely with English life, and though German, having been born in the Saxon town of Halle in 1685, he was happier living in London than in Hanover. Handel's father was a barber-surgeon, possessing no aptitude for music whatsoever. How many fathers have tried to stifle the germ of genius in their sons and failed. To George Handel Senior, music was not a respectable occupation, to him it was a kind of pedlar's calling. Yet George Frideric Handel, despite immense obstacles, was to rise to the heights in his profession. As an old man he would express a wish in the codicil to his will that the Dean and Chapter should give their permission for him to be buried "in a private manner" in Westminster Abbey.

George I was at least a good patron to Handel, increasing the £200 granted to him by Queen Anne by a further £200, though it is said that when Elector of Hanover he resented his Kappel-meister's obvious preference for London. When George I attended Handel's operas, he went incognito in a hired sedan-chair, and listened to the music from a private box. It is a sweet thought that Handel's *Water Music* was inspired by the River Thames.

The reign of George I was a period of imposing, even magnificent funerals in the Abbey. Joseph Addison, a Whig, a great essayist and master of prose, famous in his own day for his political writings in *The Spectator*, was interred on 26th June 1719. Francis Atterbury, who had been his friend and greatly admired him, though they differed in politics, officiated. Macaulay wrote in his *Essays*: "His body lay in state in the Jerusalem Chamber, and was borne to the Abbey at dead of night. Bishop Atterbury ... met the corpse, and led the procession by torchlight, round the Shrine of St Edward and the graves of the Plantagenets to the Chapel of Henry VII." The Westminster boys noticed the tenderness with which Atterbury read the lesson. In his lifetime, Addison liked to walk by himself in Westminster Abbey, easier to accomplish in the eighteenth century than in 1975. He wrote on Friday, 30th March 1711 in *The Spectator*: "When I look upon the tombs of the great, every emotion of envy dies in me; when I read the epitaphs of the beautiful, every inordinate desire goes out; ... When I read the several dates of the tombs of some that died yesterday and some six hundred years ago, I consider that great day when we shall all of us be contemporaries, and make our appearance together." Addison was very critical of Sir Cloudesley Shovel's monument in the south aisle. Shovel, a distinguished admiral, became Commander of the Fleet, lost his life in his flagship which was wrecked off the Scilly Isles in 1707. Actually a fisherman's wife confessed to ending Sir Cloudesley's life for the sake of an emerald ring. Addison wanted a more simple monument, instead "he is represented on his tomb by the figure of a Beau, dress'd in a long perriwig in reposing himself upon velvet cushions under a canopy of state". However, recent research has proved that the sculptor of this monument was Grinling Gibbons.

In 1722, there died perhaps the greatest soldier in British history, John Churchill, Duke of Marlborough, and he was given a magnificent funeral in the Abbey. Bishop Atterbury could never forgive 'Duke John' for his Whiggery, and it is unlikely that he was much affected by this solemn occasion. Alexander Pope, an intimate friend of Atterbury's who delighted in the society of writers, wrote to the Dean of Westminster on 27th July: "I intend to lie at the Deanery, and moralise one evening with you on the vanity of human glory." To which Atterbury replied: "I go tomorrow to the Deanery, and I believe, shall stay there till I have said 'Dust to Dust', and shut up that last scene of pompous vanity." The College of Heralds were mainly responsible for the arrangements, but the Dean suggested that Dr William Croft should compose some solemn music for the Burial Service. Amidst scenes of martial pomp, the procession moved along St James's Park to Hyde Park Corner, and by way of Piccadilly and Charing Cross to Westminster Abbey. John, second Duke of Montagu, was chief mourner. The coffin was lowered into a vault at the east end of Henry VII's Chapel. Over twenty years afterwards Marlborough's body was removed to Blenheim Palace in Oxfordshire, to a mausoleum, so that the victor of Blenheim might lie by the side of his beloved Sarah, his widowed Duchess.

Jacobitism to Atterbury, wrote his biographer Beeching, was only a necessary development of Toryism. It was about 1717 that the Dean of Westminster first started a correspondence with 'James III', who was then in Italy. An Irishman named George Kelly was at this period the Bishop of Rochester's chaplain, and Atterbury made use of this man for this confidential correspondence. Unfortunately, the Earl of Mar, James's treacherous adviser, betrayed Atterbury's secret activities to friends of George I's able prime minister. Sir Robert Walpole

The tomb of George Villiers, first Duke of Buckingham, together with his Duchess, by Le Sueur

Thomas Sprat, Bishop of Rochester and Dean of Westminster, and his son Thomas Sprat, Archdeacon of Rochester. Engraving after Dahl

Francis Atterbury, Dean of Westminster and Bishop of Rochester
(After Kneller)

respected the Dean of Westminster's scholarship, and he had found his opposition to the Government very embarrassing.

It is related that Sir Robert visited Atterbury at the Deanery where he tried to bribe him with the next offer of the Bishopric of Winchester. He contemptuously refused it. During August 1722 Atterbury was sitting in the Deanery in his nightgown at the unusual hour of 2 p.m. when he was arrested by Government officers. He was imprisoned in the Tower. Proceedings in Parliament by means of Bills of Pains and Penalties were brought against him, and he was banished the realm. After his trial, Atterbury asked permission to go to Westminster Abbey to see the beautiful rose window which had been erected under his supervision, but it was denied him. During the last ten years in exile, Atterbury's heart remained constantly at Westminster, and though he served "The King Over The Water" while in exile in Paris and Montpelier, his life was plagued by gout and saddened by ill health.

Atterbury died in 1732, and his body was brought back to Westminster Abbey to be interred in a family vault near the great west door. For one day his coffin remained in the workmen's lumber-room, an insult to a man of great character and ability, who lacked judgement. Dr Wilcocks, then Dean of Westminster, wanted to officiate at the funeral, but was warned that this would not be acceptable to George II's court. So Atterbury lies in peace, interred as he had desired "as far from Kings and Kaisers as the space will admit of".

Godfrey Kneller is the only illustrious painter to be commemorated in Westminster Abbey by a monument, though he is buried in Twickenham Parish Church where he was a church warden. Alexander Pope told an amusing anecdote about his friend Kneller. He had no love for Westminster: "By God, I will not be buried in Westminster!" he said emotionally. When asked why, the German retorted, "They do bury fools there." Pope composed his epitaph, one of his rare bad poems.

It was during the reign of George I in 1725 that Sir Robert Walpole reconstructed the most honourable Order of the Bath, as it was now known. On 11th May Letters Patent were passed under the Great Seal, creating a new order of knighthood. It was described in these Letters Patent as a regular military order, but as it developed during these years it was far from being a military organization. According to John Anstis Garter, King of Arms, an eminent authority on its history, Walpole used it solely for his political purposes. It is said that Sir Robert had been so often pestered by people importuning him for the Order of the Garter, that he instituted the Most Honourable Order of the Bath.

On one occasion, according to Dean Stanley, he offered it to Sarah, Duchess of Marlborough, and that difficult lady had abruptly retorted: "No, nothing but the Garter." "Madam," said the Prime Minister, "they who take the Bath will the sooner have the Garter." The first Great Master was Charles Montagu, Earl of Halifax, an important statesman and founder of the Bank of England. At the same time the Dean of Westminster was made Dean of the Order. The number of Knights, which was thirty to sixty, corresponded with the number of stalls in the Henry VII Chapel. It was in 1725 that the Henry VII Chapel was first used for installations of the Knights of the Bath, and it is still so used today. The most important ceremony recently to take place there was the installation by Her Majesty the Queen of her son the Prince of Wales as Great Master on 28th May 1975, when he succeeded his great-uncle the late Duke of Gloucester in that office.

It is still the custom on 20th October, the anniversary of George I's coronation, for the Knights of the Bath in their robes of oyster satin with scarlet linings, to take part in a service in the Henry VII Chapel. Formerly as the Knights filed out of the great west door of the Abbey, the royal master cook, usually a bulky aproned man armed with a formidable chopping knife, stood there to warn the Knights that if they betrayed their vows, he would hack off their spurs. A scene depicting this was painted by Canaletto for Bishop Wilcocks in 1747, and is now in the Dean's house.

Sir Isaac Newton, born in 1642 at Woolsthorpe near Grantham in Lincolnshire, was undoubtedly one of our greatest scientists. He died during the early months of 1727 in his eighty-sixth year. Among the vast congregation present at his funeral in the Abbey was his warm admirer Voltaire, who said of Newton: "Of all the geniuses of the universe assembled he should lead the band." Newton's body first lay in state in the Jerusalem Chamber.

Attended by members of the Royal Society, his remains were interred in front of the choir screen. On the gravestone are the words: "*Hic depositum est quod mortale fuit Isaac Newtoni.*" (Here lies what was mortal of Isaac Newton). People often ask for Newton, but he is not as great an attraction as David Livingstone, who is interred in the nave.

In 1727, George I, lonely and unloved, embarked for Hanover together with his ugly old mistress, the Duchess of Kendal, and in the course of the journey was seized with a sudden illness, culminating in his death. It is surely more appropriate that the King should be buried in his beloved Hanover and not in Westminster Abbey.

It was characteristic of the Hanoverian Kings to dislike their sons, and George I had quarrelled with his son, who succeeded him as George II. An irascible, fiery, profligate little man, he was at least fortunate in his Queen Caroline of Anspach. So much more intelligent than himself.

It was at George II's coronation on 11th October that Handel composed four magnificent anthems. Lord Harvey has described the scene in his memoirs: "The ceremony was performed with all the pomp and magnificence that could be contrived, the present King differing so much from the last that all the pageantry and splendour, badges and trappings of royalty were as pleasing to the son as they were irksome to the father. The dress of the Queen Caroline on this occasion was as fine as the accumulated riches of the city and suburbs could make it; for besides her own jewels (which were a great number and very valuable) she had on her head and on her shoulders all the pearls she could borrow of the ladies of quality at one end of the town, and on her petticoat all the diamonds she could hire of the Jews and jewellers at the other ..."

George II's knowledge of music did not amount to much, but he increased Handel's pension another £200 per annum for his services as music master to his daughters Princesses Amelia and Caroline. Since his father favoured the composer, Frederick, Prince of Wales showed his hostility to Handel by intriguing against him. It is very much to King George's credit that he supported Handel in no uncertain terms against the ill-mannered postures of the Prince of Wales.

Westminster Abbey belongs to every age. Sir Christopher Wren, had been appointed Fabric Surveyor by the Dean and Chapter during 1698, and was responsible for designing the lower portion of the western towers, which seem to dominate the building from a distance. The great architect had several ambitions, the erection of a lofty spire, which might render the whole fabric more graceful, the completion of the two western towers and lastly to make the north front more magnificent. Wren, however, had died in 1723 aged ninety-one and it was his pupil Nicholas Hawksmoor, who completed the work during George II's reign. Wren's model, which is preserved in a poor condition in the Abbey, shows the height to which he intended to carry up the tower. Alas, the architect's proposed lofty spire was never built.

Hawksmoor was created surveyor general of Westminster Abbey and continued to work at the two western towers. Indeed his influence on the designs of many churches of the period has been underrated. A very modest man, his temper remained serene, despite severe bouts of gout. Dr Joseph Wilcock had succeeded Dean Bradford in 1731, and while Dean of Westminster the western towers were completed.

Caroline of Anspach predeceased her husband, dying in great agony in 1737. When the Queen implored her husband to marry again, George II, who had been constantly unfaithful, choking to drown his sorrow mumbled, "Non, non, j'aurai des maitresses." Caroline, described by Dean Stanley as a discriminating patroness of learning and philosophy, was the last Queen consort to be interred in the Abbey.

It was Handel who composed an inspired anthem for Caroline's funeral, "When the Ear Heard Her, Then it Blessed Her; and When the Eye Saw Her, it Gave Witness to Her". The Bishop of Chichester wrote to his son: "The procession went into Henry VII's Chapel. Princess Amelia was the chief mourner ... The funeral service was performed by the Bishop of Rochester, as Dean of Westminster." He wrote that the music set by Mr Handel was considered to be as good a piece as he ever composed, and that it was about fifty minutes in singing.

George Frideric Handel had lived in London for thirty-six years until his death in 1759, at a house then 47 Lower Brook

Street off Hanover Street. The *Whitehall Evening Post* relates during April: "Last night about eight o'clock the remains of the late, great Mr Handel were deposited at the foot of the Duke of Argyle's statue ... almost the greatest concourse of people of all ranks ever seen upon such, or indeed upon any other occasion." The gentlemen of His Majesty's Chapels Royal, and the choirs of St Paul's and St Peter's (Westminster) attended the obsequies and sang Dr Croft's Funeral Anthem. It is appropriate that Handel, a genius, who had delighted in the society of the poets, and had much of the poet in his nature, should be interred in Poets' Corner. In his will Handel had left £600 to pay for the monument erected in his memory. Louis François Roubiliac was the French sculptor, but the statue has been criticized as unimaginative, though contemporaries considered it a noble work. Roubiliac was a protégé of Walpole, and lived in England for thirty years. Handel stands with the score of the *Messiah* in his hand, and the inscription above his monument is: "I know that my redeemer liveth". How pleasant to watch the wrapt faces of our visitors to the Abbey as they gaze at Roubiliac's monument.

George II is the last of our sovereigns to be interred in the Abbey. Horace Walpole, with his insatiable curiosity, found much to interest him. "When we came to the Chapel of Henry VII, all solemnity and decorum ceased; no order was observed, people sat or stood where they could or would; the Yeomen of the Guard were crying out for help, oppressed by the immense weight of the coffin ... The Duke of Newcastle fell into a fit of crying the moment he came into the Chapel ... the Archbishop hovering over him with a smelling bottle; but in two minutes his curiosity got the better of his hypocrisy, and he ran about the Chapel with his glass to spy who was or was not there ..." All George II's children, including Frederick, Prince of Wales, and William Augustus, Duke of Cumberland, 'Butcher Cumberland' – I can never forgive him for Culloden – are buried in the same vault. This period is of importance, for it marks the culmination of the Abbey's connection with the tombs of the kings and queens of England.

Zachary Pearce, when he became Dean of Westminster in 1756, had done so reluctantly for he wished to retire from his Bishopric of Bangor into private life. He was a fine scholar, but he has been criticized for his poor taste. In consenting to the erection of a monument for the much lauded General James Wolfe, killed in a heroic action whilst storming Quebec, he proposed that it should take the place of the noble tomb of Aymer de Valence, Earl of Pembroke. Horace Walpole expressed his indignation, and wrote Dr Pearce asking him to bestow the monument on him, so that he could remove it to Strawberry Hill. Fortunately the Dean changed his mind, learning that Aymer was not a wicked Knight Templar. Thank heavens he still lies serene near the high altar, separating Avelina, Countess of Lancaster from her husband Edmund Crouchback. Dean Pearce remained at Westminster until 1768, though in an interview with George III in 1761 he tried to resign the Bishopric of Rochester and as Dean of Westminster.

George III, son of Frederick, Prince of Wales (died 1751) and Princess Augusta of Saxe Gotha, succeeded his grandfather as King in 1760 when only twenty-two. Horace Walpole wrote to George Montague on 31st October, "The young King has all the appearance of being amiable. There is great grace to temper, much dignity and extreme good nature, which breaks out on all occasions." Horace Walpole wrote that George loved medals. However, he was slow, prejudiced and obstinate, though not lacking in intelligence. George married Princess Charlotte, Dowager of Mecklenburg-Strelitz. On meeting her, Walpole wrote his impressions: "She is not tall, nor a beauty, pale and very thin, but looks sensible and is genteel. Her hair is darkish and fine; her forehead low, and her nose very well, except the nostrils spreading too wide ..."

Horace Walpole's celebrated contemporary account of the King and Queen's joint coronation, written to the diplomat Horace Mann, in a letter from Strawberry Hill, remains the most entertaining description. "What is the finest sight in the world? A coronation. At a coronation one sees the peerage as exalted as they like to be, and at a trial as much humbled as a plebeian wishes them ..." There was roaring inflation at this period. At George II's coronation, Walpole's mother had given forty guineas for a dining-room, scaffold and bed-chamber. His grandson's similar apartments with a worse view cost as much as three hundred and fifty guineas. He aptly remarked that the prebends would like a coronation every year. The King paid nine thousand pounds for the hire of jewels for his Queen. The superstitious, however, were alarmed when the largest jewel fell from George's crown, an ominous incident, which was subsequently believed to have predicted the loss of America. The Queen had a retiring-chamber, with all conveniences, behind the altar in the Abbey. She was much disconcerted, however, on going there to find the Duke of Newcastle already ensconced there.

The banquet afterwards in Westminster Hall was even more splendid. Dymoke was much admired for the manner in which he performed his duties, while George and Charlotte performed their parts with majesty, and grace. The Duke of Bedford, the Earl of Effingham and the Earl of Talbot as they rode into the Hall, have been described as prancing and curveting like hobby-horses. It is said that Prince Charles Edward Stuart, James II's grandson, 'the Young Pretender', was secretly watching the scene from the gallery. Imagine the confusion if he had answered Dymoke's challenge!

One of the most magnificent monuments in the north aisle of the Henry VII Chapel, in the Abbey, is that of John Sheffield, first Duke of Buckinghamshire, who started his career at Charles II's Court. He was an enemy of the poet genius John Wilmot, Earl of Rochester, who lampooned him when he was the Earl of Mulgrave as "Monster All-Pride". John Macky in his *Memoirs of the Secret Services*, described him in his later life: "He is a nobleman of learning, and good natural parts, but of no principles. Violent for the High Church, yet seldom goes to it." John Sheffield fell into disgrace at the end of his career because of his Jacobite sympathies. His wife Catherine, who erected the monument, was the illegitimate daughter of James II by Catherine Sedley, and she died in 1743. John Sheffield more properly belongs to an earlier era, for he had once been a suitor for the hand of Princess Anne and banished the realm for his audacity.

Oliver Goldsmith, who died during the reign of George III in 1774, was not interred in the Abbey, but in the Temple Church. The author of that delightful comedy, *She Stoops to Conquer*, and of *The Vicar of Wakefield*, had a monument and tablet erected to his memory in the south transept of Poets' Corner. Many celebrated actors are interred in the Abbey, including Thomas Betterton, who delighted Restoration audiences, John Henderson, considered second only to Garrick in his own day. Mrs Oldfield interred in the nave beneath Congreve's elegant monument, and David Garrick himself, one of the greatest actors. Garrick, born in Hereford in 1716, died at Adelphi Terrace in 1779. His funeral on 1st February was attended by most of the leading literary, artistic and political personalities of the age: "I saw old Samuel Johnson" said Richard Cumberland, the dramatist "standing at the foot of Shakespeare's monument, and bathed in tears." It was right, too, that Dr Samuel Johnson, a great writer, author of the *Lives of the Poets* and the *Dictionary* of the English language, should be interred in the Abbey near the foot of Shakespeare's monument. Shakespeare, of course, is buried in Stratford-on-Avon, but his monument in the Abbey was erected in 1740. On the scroll are some lines from *The Tempest*. William Wordsworth, greatest of the Lake poets, is buried in Grasmere, though there is a seated statue of him in the Abbey. Mrs Alphra Behn a novelist and first woman to turn to playwriting as a profession, was buried there in 1689.

Richard Brinsley Sheridan, whose ambitions were political rather than literary, was interred, too, in the Abbey when he died in July 1816. He would have protested against being laid to rest in Poets' Corner, but it is fitting that he should be buried near Garrick. Sheridan's immortality is owing to his brilliance as a dramatist, not to his eloquence as a politician. Sheridan, who died in dire poverty, was given a lavish funeral. His body was first borne to Peter Moore's house in Great George Street, Westminster. Among the pall-bearers were Lord Holland, the Duke of Bedford, Lords Lauderdale and Spencer. It is sad that Sheridan's inscription is becoming more and more dilapidated.

No doubt Sheridan would have preferred to be near his friend, the Whig statesman Charles James Fox, interred in the north transept in 1806. Fox's monument is now in the north-west angle of the nave. It is by Westmacott and represents Fox dying in the arms of Liberty, while a negro at his feet shows his gratitude for Fox's share in abolishing the slave trade. By chance, when visiting St Peter's Church, Chertsey, on a summer day, I was delighted to find a plaque commemorating him. It is curious the way rivals are often buried close together in the Abbey, and the great William Pitt the Younger, Prime Minister at twenty-four, lies near Fox. His monument is also by Westmacott, seeming to dominate the west door, for the great man holds his audience spell-bound, while the forces of anarchy – the French Revolution – are depicted vanquished at his feet. One remembers his last recorded words: "Oh! My Country! How I leave my Country." Britain in 1806 faced terrible problems as she does today.

William Pitt was the younger son of William Pitt, Earl of Chatham, an eminent statesman, who died in 1778. As Dean Stanley relates, his body was brought from the Painted Chamber in Westminster, and interred in the centre of the north transept. He was born in Westminster. Tall and imposing, he gave an impression of majesty, and he had the eyes of a hawk, and a long aquiline nose. The north transept, or statesman's aisle, is the burial place of the great parliamentarians, as the south transept, or Poets' Corner opposite contains the monuments of poets, scholars and others. Chatham's monument is by the sculptor John Bacon, and an amusing story is related of George III and Bacon. The King approved of it, but told him: "Now Bacon, mind you don't turn author, but stick to your chisel."

It was considered such an honour to be buried in Westminster Abbey that Horatio Nelson, upon going into action at the Battle of the Nile, exclaimed: "Before this time tomorrow I shall have gained a peerage, or Westminster Abbey." Dean Stanley, however, maintains that Nelson said: "Westminster Abbey or glorious victory," at the Battle of Cape St Vincent, (4th February 1797). Nelson was interred in St Paul's Cathedral in 1805, and the wax effigy, now in the Abbey museum was made a year later, to attract visitors back to the Abbey, who were deserting Westminster for St Paul's. Two years before his death at Trafalgar, Nelson was installed by proxy as a Knight of the Bath, in May 1803. His successor was Sir Arthur Wellesley, later Duke of Wellington.

Occasionally gross injustices have occurred. One such case concerned Thomas Cochrane, later Earl of Dundonald, a celebrated admiral, who helped Chile achieve her freedom.

Accused of fraud in 1814, his name was struck off the rolls of the Knights of the Bath. Actually the only grounds for degradation are provided in Article III of the Statutes. They are for heresy, cowardice, and for the more heinous offence of high treason. It was therefore necessary for the Prince Regent to direct a royal warrant to the Dean of Westminster, countersigned by Lord Sidmouth, the Home Secretary. To complete his disgrace, Cochrane's banner was taken from its place in the Henry VII Chapel, and flung down the steps. Much to the honour of the Prince Consort, who wanted to right a flaming injustice, the tenth Earl of Dundonald (as he became) was later readmitted to the ranks of the Order. In 1860, on the day of Dundonald's funeral, Queen Victoria ordered that the banner of the great sailor should be restored to its former position. A celebrated soldier, Sir Eyre Coote was similarly degraded and expelled in 1816, but he died unaware that he would later be rehabilitated.

George III is a tragic personality, a victim of fits of insanity, living in Windsor Castle. His death in 1820 marks the final separation of royal burials from Westminster Abbey. This was partly owing to growing lack of space, but also due to the King's intimate association with Windsor for so many years. George III and Queen Charlotte were interred at Windsor together with many of their children, including the two youngest Alfred and Octavius, who had been removed from George II's vault in the Abbey.

Of the outstanding Deans during George III's reign, John Thomas was devoted to music, and it was during his tenure of the Deanery that a new choir was built. He took the initiative in organizing the great Handel memorial festival in 1784. His successor, Samuel Horsley, has been described in *A House of Kings* as the most distinguished Dean since Atterbury, and he was an eloquent preacher, especially when he depicted very vividly the contemporary scene in France after Louis XVI and Marie Antoinette had been guillotined. His mastery of the English language impressed his listeners in the Abbey. His successor William Vincent was passionately interested in the restoration of the Henry VII Chapel.

The new King George IV, who succeeded his father in 1820, loved pomp and display. He enjoyed the ritual of his coronation, which took place on 19th July 1821. He was twenty minutes late because his Lord Great Chamberlain, Lord Gwydyr had torn his clothes whilst getting ready for the ceremony. As George IV joined the procession moving towards the Abbey from Westminster Hall, he was a resplendent figure, seeming to the peeresses and the foreign ambassadors like some gorgeous bird of paradise. His train of crimson velvet shone with gold stars, and his black Spanish hat might have been severe if it had not been for its great plumes of white ostrich feathers. The procession was headed for the last time in its history by the King's herb-woman and her six attendants scattering herbs on the way. As George entered the Abbey he was greeted by the Hallelujah Chorus. The King's demeanour during the ceremony can hardly be described as reverent, for he appeared inattentive. He was seen to nod, wink and sigh and to make eyes at Lady Conyngham, one of his mistresses. The portly King found the heat extremely trying, and at one stage had to be revived by smelling salts given him by the Archbishop of Canterbury's Secretary. His coronation, lasting for five hours, was certainly an ordeal. Dr Harcourt, Archbishop of York, preached a sermon in which he made veiled allusions to the King's lax morals. There was every need for the good ruler to preserve his subjects' morals from the contagion of vice and irreligion. Dean Ireland of Westminster officiated.

George's wife, Queen Caroline of Brunswick-Wolfenbuttel tried to obtain entrance into Westminster Abbey, but was peremptorily refused. She retired in dudgeon, dying later in the same year, to be buried in Brunswick.

The coronation banquet was a splendid affair. The Lord High Constable, the Duke of Wellington, the Lord High Steward, the Marquis of Anglesey and the Deputy Earl Marshal, Lord Howard of Effingham, rode about Westminster Hall. For the last time the hereditary King's Champion, the twenty-year-old son of the Reverend John Dymoke, a rector in Lincolnshire, flung down his gauntlet three times. Nobody took up the challenge. As was customary the King drank to his Champion from a gold cup. The 312 fortunate guests no doubt enjoyed the tasty dishes, such as lobster and crayfish and goose (eighty dishes). George's coronation was a very extravagant affair, for it cost £240,000 in contrast with his younger brother William IV's £30,000.

George IV's character was mixed. He was called "the first gentleman of Europe", but he was capable of rudeness and coarseness. On occasions he behaved callously to friends, but he was clever, versatile and an amusing conversationalist. His morals were very bad, yet it was the Prince Regent who had the good taste to have erected in St Peter's in Rome the monument by Canova, to commemorate the tragic Stuarts. When Spencer Percevel, the Prime Minister[1] was assassinated in the House of Commons in May 1812, the Prince Regent together with Parliament had a handsome monument erected to commemorate him.

If George's tastes were extravagant, his brother William's were very simple. William, Duke of Clarence, succeeded his brother as William IV in 1830. He had served as a naval officer for many years, and he was bluff, tactless and detested all ceremonial display. William in fact objected to his coronation. His historical sense was wholly lacking, and he was unable to appreciate the mysticism or the solemnity of the occasion. As his biographer Philip Ziegler states, he regarded it as a pointless piece of flummery. Economy was absolutely essential, yet it was to be deplored that the customary banquet was not held in Westminster Hall. Consequently William's coronation was derisively referred to as "the Half Coronation". Princess Marie Louise in her book *My Memory of Six Reigns*, relates that the Duchess of Kent had tactlessly demanded that her brother-in-law, the King, should allow her daughter, Princess Victoria, then a child of eleven, and heir presumptive, to have her own special procession to the Abbey. William refused on the grounds that Queen Adelaide might yet have a large family. "Very well," said the Duchess, "then she will not go at all." William and Adelaide were crowned together in the Abbey on 8th September 1831. Lady Wharncliffe wrote: "The King was very infirm in his walk, poor man, and looked oppress'd with the immense weight of his robes and crown." When he was being disrobed for the anointing, Archbishop Howley was flabbergasted to discover that the King was wearing the full-dress uniform of an Admiral of the Fleet. Those who visit Loseley Park near Guildford, the

[1] The only prime minister so far to be assassinated in the House of Commons.

Tudor home of the More-Molyneux family, are shown William IV's coronation chair, in which the King rested during the ceremony, though no doubt he was crowned in Edward I's coronation chair. Mr James More-Molyneux informed me that this chair is always presented to the Dean of Westminster before a coronation. Dean Ireland officiated, as he had done at George IV's coronation.

Greatly admired were the Earl Marshal's pages resplendent in their blue frock coats, white breeches and stockings, a crimson silk sash and hats curiously ill-shaped with an ostrich feather. Among the foreign ambassadors the carriage of Prince Esterhazy was the most splendid.

King William died on 20th June 1837, and was succeeded by his niece Queen Victoria, now eighteen. Throughout her long life, Victoria had two great virtues, her dedicated sense of duty and her strong religious faith in God, even as a girl.

Victoria wrote her own account of her coronation day, 28th June 1838, in her diary. "I was awoke at four o'clock by the guns in the Park, and could not get much sleep afterwards on account of the noise of the people, bands, etc., etc. Got up at seven, feeling strong and well; the Park presented a curious spectacle, crowds of people up to Constitution Hill, soldiers, bands, etc.

"At ten I got into the State Coach with the Duchess of Sutherland and Lord Albemarle and we began our progress ... I reached the Abbey amid deafening cheers at a little after half past eleven." The Queen's eight train-bearers, including Lady Caroline Lennox, Lady Adelaide Paget, and Lady Mary Grimston, were all beautifully dressed in white satin, and pink roses in the trimming of their dresses.

Felix Mendelssohn, the famous composer, an eye witness, deeply impressed by the blare of trumpets, the pealing of church bells and the roar of guns, wrote that one had to pinch oneself to make sure it was not all a dream out of the *Arabian Nights*.

There are delightful little touches about the Queen's Prime Minister, Lord Melbourne, which reveal her affection for him. He told her that Edward Maltby, Bishop of Durham, who should have instructed her on the procedure during this momentous day, was remarkably maladroit. "He never could tell me what was to take place," wrote the Queen. When the Crown was placed on Victoria's head by Archbishop Howley, "a most beautiful, impressive moment" for the Queen, Lord Melbourne, who stood very close to the Queen throughout the whole ceremony, was completely overcome, and very much affected: "He gave *such* a kind, and I may say *fatherly* look." As the Queen was crowned this was the signal for the peers and peeresses to put on their coronets. There were the incidents which lingered in her memory: "Poor old Lord Rolle," aged eighty-two and extremely infirm, making the effort to ascend the steps to make the customary homage, only to fall down. The Queen courteously walked to the end of the steps to prevent him falling again. Lord Melbourne, Lord Grey and the Duke of Wellington all paid their homage. The moment, which impressed her most was "when my good Lord Melbourne knelt down and kissed my hand, he pressed my hand and I grasped his with all my heart, at which he looked up with eyes filled with tears and seemed much touched, as he was, I observed, throughout the whole ceremony".

Lord Melbourne, a natural sceptic, thought that St Edward's Chapel was more unlike a Chapel than anything he had ever seen; "for what was *called* an *Altar* was covered with sandwiches, bottles of wine, etc., etc." As the elderly statesman felt extremely tired he drank a glass of wine. Archbishop Howley seems to have been as maladroit as the Bishop of Durham, for he put the ring on Victoria's wrong finger, causing her considerable pain when she wrenched it off. Victoria's coronation was inefficiently organized, and there was much confusion. Dr John Ireland, Dean of Westminster, was very unwell, and unable to attend. His place was taken by the sub-Dean, Lord John Thynne.

No longer the coronation banquet in Westminster Hall, but the relaxed atmosphere of a dinner party at Buckingham Palace attended by the Queen, her relations and Lord Melbourne. Victoria enjoyed the entertaining conversation of Melbourne, telling her that the Archbishop's and Dean's copes, both remarkably handsome, were worn at James II's coronation. He laughed when telling her of the enormous breakfast he had enjoyed before the ceremony in the Jerusalem Chamber. "Whenever the clergy, or a Dean and Chapter, had anything to do with anything, there's sure to be plenty to eat." The Queen ended the day by looking at the fireworks in Green Park from a balcony, and she thought them quite beautiful.

The tragedy of Queen Victoria's life was the death of her beloved husband, Albert the Prince Consort, who had never been robust, in December 1861. Among the ladies attending the Queen was Lady Augusta Bruce, daughter of the Earl of Elgin, a friend of Victoria's, who later married the celebrated Arthur Penrhyn Stanley, Dean of Westminster. Lady Augusta records the Queen's agony and her anxiety about Great Britain in a letter to her brother: "The Country, oh the Country." Victoria's emotional nature gave her no respite. The Queen grew very attached to Lady Augusta.

Arthur Penrhyn Stanley was truly a great Victorian, a man whose influence pervades the Abbey even today. He travelled widely in Europe and the Near East. It was in 1862 that this distinguished scholar was chosen to accompany Edward, Prince of Wales on a tour to Egypt, Palestine and other countries. This led on his return to England to a friendship with Queen Victoria, and her family. Mixing in Court circles he made the acquaintance of Lady Augusta Bruce, and the friendship ripened to love. During November 1863, Stanley received a letter from the Prime Minister, Lord Palmerston, offering him the Deanery of Westminster now vacant by the promotion of Doctor Trench to the Archbishropric of Dublin. He married Lady Augusta in the Abbey during December, and he was installed on 8th January 1864. It was the Dean of Westminster who officiated at the marriage of Victoria's younger son, Alfred, Duke of Edinburgh, to the Grand Duchess Marie Alexandrovna of St Petersburg during 1874. The Stanleys stayed sometimes with the Queen at Osborne in the Isle of Wight and her other houses.

Dean Stanley succeeded in his ambition to make Westminster Abbey more and more the centre of religious and national life, and he eagerly encouraged special services there. He was passionately interested in the monuments, and readers of *Historical Memorials of Westminster Abbey* cannot fail but be impressed by Stanley's powers of description, and his ability to make those who are interred in their tombs, truly alive. For him they were not dead relics, but glowing and gloriously alive. How can all those Kings, Queens, servants, poets, statesmen, scientists, musicians and abbots be dead when their names and exploits are so constantly on the lips of vergers and guides? That is why the Abbey is so exciting. Standing in the medieval cloisters, alone on an autumn evening, while the Abbey lamps dimly flicker, one almost senses the presence of the Benedictine monks, who once walked on its pavements.

Owing to lack of space, Stanley warmly supported the reluctance of his immediate predecessors to sanction burials in the Abbey. Sir Rowland Hill, commemorated for his penny postage, was interred in the Chapel of St Paul in 1879, while nine years earlier Charles Dickens was buried secretly in the Poets' Corner, with only a dozen mourners present. On the other hand, an enormous crowd assembled for the funeral of David Livingstone, whose body was borne to London from Zanzibar and interred in the Abbey in April 1894. Livingstone's tablet in the nave attracts thousands of our home and overseas visitors. Thomas Babington Macaulay, a very eminent historian, though prejudiced, and a fine master of narrative, is interred near Addison in the north aisle. Earlier, during the reign of William IV, William Wilberforce, the philanthropist, whose name will always be associated with the abolition of slavery, was given a stately funeral in the north transept.

A story is told of Dean Stanley and of Benjamin Disraeli, Earl of Beaconsfield, a favourite of the Queen's and William Gladstone's great rival. Walking one day towards Westminster Abbey, Stanley met by chance Disraeli, then Prime Minister, in Whitehall. "My head is full of telegrams. Will you allow me to take a turn with you, and get some fresh air?" asked Disraeli. They entered the Abbey by the north transept and listened to Canon Farrar's fine sermon about the length of eternity. The Dean showed his friend the best way to slip out of the Abbey without being observed. When Disraeli died in 1881, Stanley was very anxious to find space for the erection of a monument commemorating the Tory statesman, but it is evident from the *First Report of the Royal Commission Appointed to Inquire Into the Present Want of Space for Monuments in Westminster Abbey*, 1890, that there were difficulties. Dean Stanley was in fact bitterly disappointed that Beaconsfield was not interred in the Abbey, but at his family home at Hughenden in Buckinghamshire. The

Queen explained the reason when writing to Dean Stanley: "I know he would wish to rest with the wife he loved so well, and not in Westminster Abbey, where, however, I am anxious that a monument should be erected to his memory." It is fitting that Disraeli should be next to Gladstone in the Statesman's Aisle, rivals in life and so utterly dissimilar in character. Gladstone and his wife Catherine were, however, interred in the Abbey many years later.

Henry John Temple, third Viscount Palmerston, was another eminent Victorian, a man both beloved by his contemporaries and disliked by others for the impression of levity he conveyed. 'Pam' as he was affectionately called, or 'Cupid' as he was nicknamed, was certainly a lover of the fair sex and none too scrupulous in pursuing his quarry. There was a grandeur about 'Pam' sadly missing in our politicians today. His marriage to his old love, Lady Cowper (the widowed Lord Melbourne's sister), when they were both over fifty, was a great success, though the Queen opposed it. 'Pam' was a prodigious worker whilst Foreign Secretary and later as Prime Minister, but it is scarcely surprising if he quarrelled with the Queen and the Prince Consort, though later harmony reigned. Lord Palmerston died in 1865, and he was interred in the Abbey. A statue in his honour was erected by Parliament. There he stands, proud and boastful, and jealous of the rights of Englishmen. As a young man he had travelled in Italy, and supported that country which he loved in its struggles for unification. Four years later Lady Palmerston was buried in her husband's grave in the north transept.

Near Gladstone and Disraeli is the monument of Sir Robert Peel, a Prime Minister who worked in harmony with the Prince Consort. The metropolitan police were named after him 'Bobbies', but Peel was interred according to his wish at Drayton and not in Westminster Abbey.

Queen Victoria seldom attended services in the Abbey, but she showed her sympathy for Dean Stanley by her presence there at Lady Augusta's funeral in 1876, seated in the so-called "Abbot's Pew", looking down on the south side of the western end of the Nave. Victoria considered the service was too long. There were many humble people in the congregation for the lady was much beloved. Among the pall-bearers were the Duke of Westminster,

Lord Shaftesbury the philanthropist, and Mr Campbell Bannerman then Member of Parliament for Dunfermline, who as Sir Henry Campbell-Bannerman was to become a distinguished Prime Minister during the reign of Edward VII.

Lady Augusta's husband, Dean Stanley, survived her five years, and the Queen gave permission that he should be interred in the Henry VII Chapel. His helpmate, the devoted Lady Augusta, rests in a vault beneath Stanley's coffin.

It was no easy task to succeed a man of the calibre of Dean Stanley, but George Granville Bradley served with distinction as Dean of Westminster for over twenty years. Much of the time he was engrossed with administrative matters. Dean Bradley held office for two occasions of national importance, the Golden Jubilee service of 1887 marking fifty years of Victoria's reign, and the state funeral of the grand old man William Ewart Gladstone almost at the end of the era in 1898.

Queen Victoria's carriage slowly wended its way on 20th June from Buckingham Palace to Westminster Abbey. Victoria's face betrayed both pride and emotion as the cheering of her subjects roused her consciousness like the surge of waves beating on a shore. Seated beside her were the lovely Princess Alexandra, the Danish Princess who had married her son the Prince of Wales, and the Crown Princess of Germany, the beloved Princess Royal, 'Vicky' of the early years. Vicky's husband Fritz was described "sitting his charger as proudly as a medieval knight", and beaming with delight at the applause he received. What memories must have crowded the Queen's mind in the Abbey. If only Albert could have seen her triumph, how joyful he would have been, and Lord Melbourne, too, so long ago paying homage to her, his young Queen, with tears in his eyes. At her Golden Jubilee service the Queen did not wear her crown or robes of state.

The less agreeable aspects of Victoria's character are depicted in her relations with the great Prime Minister, William Ewart Gladstone, whom she personally disliked. However, it is fair to add that Gladstone handled her badly. Victoria's chief faults were her violent prejudices, probably inherited from her German ancestors, her maddening obstinacy and her over-emotional nature.

When the Prince of Wales acted as pall-bearer at Gladstone's funeral in Westminster Abbey in 1898, and gently kissed Mrs Gladstone's hand after the service, the Queen was very annoyed. The Prince and Princess of Wales had both been staunch friends of Gladstone. Alexandra described Gladstone in a letter to his wife Catherine as "that great and good man whose name will go down in letters of gold to posterity as one of the most beautiful upright and disinterested characters that has ever adorned the pages of history". Alexandra herself attended the service, in the Abbey. A little crucifix, which had belonged to the Gladstones, hung always beside the Princess's bed. Earlier, loving friends had kept vigil over Gladstone's bier as his body lay in state in Westminster Hall and the silent multitudes filed past.

Among the distinguished Great Masters of the Most Honourable Order of the Bath was Prince Arthur of Connaught, Queen Victoria's youngest and favourite son, appointed Grand Master on 26th February 1901. He filled the office with distinction for several decades. His mother had recently died at Osborne, to be at last united with her beloved Albert in the mausoleum at Frogmore. It was the end of an era.

Edward, Prince of Wales, who succeeded his mother on the throne in January 1901, as Edward VII*, was a man of great charm and tact, and possessed rare qualities as a diplomat. He was now in his sixtieth year. Owing to the King's serious illness, his coronation, originally arranged for 26th June 1902, was postponed. Edward VII was keenly interested in etiquette and ceremonial, and took much interest in all the details of his coronation. Now that she was Queen Consort, Alexandra was determined to wear exactly what she liked, "and so shall my ladies" she said, for she refused to be bound by precedents, set up by William IV's Queen Adelaide seventy-one years earlier. The material for Alexandra's dress was embroidered in India, and the Viceroy Lord Curzon's American wife closely supervised the work. Her crimson velvet state robes were hand-woven at Braintree in Essex.

The coronation was finally fixed for Saturday, 9th August

* Edward VII was not a Hanoverian King. As the son of Albert, the Prince Consort, he belonged to the house of Saxe-Coburg-Gotha.

1902. It was related by the late Duke of Windsor that Edward
VII's Danish Queen, who was notoriously unpunctual, kept her
husband waiting until the King, who could hardly conceal his
annoyance, told her: "My dear Alix, if you don't come
immediately, you won't be crowned Queen." To spare the King
extra fatigue, the service in the Abbey was much shortened. For
instance, the homage usually performed severally by all the peers
was done by the Archbishop of Canterbury on behalf of the
Lords Spiritual, and the senior of each degree acted on behalf of
the Lords Temporal. The sermon was omitted altogether, and the
Bishops of Bath and Wells, and Oxford sang the Litany on the
steps of Henry VII's Chapel before the arrival of the royal
procession. The Chapter of Westminster arranged for the regalia
to be brought from the Jerusalem Chamber where it had been
overnight to St Edwards Chapel behind the high altar.

No unseemly incidents married Edward VII's coronation. Dr
Bradley was too infirm to undertake all the functions devolving
on the Dean, consequently the sub-Dean Duckworth played a
prominent part in assisting Dean Bradley. The Archbishop of
Canterbury at this period was the aged Dr Frederick Temple.
Edward VII's earlier illness made him more sensitive as to the
infirmities of the elderly prelate, who was to crown him. It must
be emphasized that Dr Maclagan, Archbishop of York, had no
traditional or proven right to crown Queen Alexandra, but he
was chosen by the sovereign. He had served as a soldier. Among
the bishops in the procession was Bishop Davidson of
Winchester, an intimate friend of Queen Victoria's, who many
considered would succeed Temple at Canterbury. The sword of
state was borne by Lord Londonderry, the grand-nephew of the
distinguished statesman Robert Stewart, Viscount Castlereagh,
(later Marquis of Londonderry) whose mighty endeavours had
helped to secure the peace of Europe after Napoleon had been
vanquished. The Duke of Norfolk held the baton of the Earl
Marshal, and it is the hereditary right of the Howards to act in
this capacity. The Duke of Marlborough had the honour of
carrying the imperial crown.

Many spectators in the Abbey watched nervously as old
Temple, standing in front of his King, seated in St Edward's
Chair, carefully lifted the crown from the cushion on which it

was held by the sub-Dean Duckworth. For one terrible moment of suspense the Archbishop seemed to falter, then set the imperial crown on Edward VII's head. The trumpets sounded, and the voices of the choir singing the *Confortari* could be heard in the still air. Archbishop Temple, deeply impressed by the occasion, recited the formula of homage, saying: "God bless you, Sir; God be with you, Sir." Then arousing himself, the old man attemped to kiss the King's cheek, but Edward always kindly, and considerate, took hold of his hands, but Temple would have fallen had it not been for the vigilance of the Bishop of Winchester. The Abbey was filled with lovely women, such as the American-born Duchess of Marlborough, the Duchesses of Portland, Montrose, and Sutherland, but none surpassed Queen Alexandra in her beauty and radiance. Asked by his doctor, Sir Frederick Treves, what had impressed him most, Edward replied that it was the simultaneous movement of the peeresses in putting on their coronets. "Their white arms arching over their heads had suggested inevitably a ballet," explained the King.

Dean Bradley did not survive the coronation long, dying in 1903. He was succeeded by an eccentric scholar Armitage Robinson, described by Canon Fox in *A House of Kings* as "an impressive and picturesque figure" deeply interested in the history of the Abbey. He was a striking personality and after he vacated his post he returned to the Abbey several times to fulfil the function of Lord High Almoner at the distribution of the Royal Maundy.

The famous actor Sir Henry Irving died in 1905 during the short reign of Edward VII, and he was interred near Garrick in Poets' Corner. It was Irving with his great sonorous voice who produced several of Alfred Lord Tennyson's historical plays on the stage. Tennyson and Robert Browning belong to the Victorian age, and they were both buried in the Abbey. Tennyson's poem "Crossing the Bar" was first sung at the Poet Laureate's funeral in 1892. Elizabeth Barrett Browning died in 1861, and she was buried in her beloved Florence, where she had lived for many years. So united in life to her fellow poet and husband Robert Browning, their bodies at last were separated in death. Browning died in Venice and his remains were brought to the Abbey to be interred near Chaucer's monument.

BIBLIOGRAPHY

Anstis, "Observations Introductory to an Historical Essay upon the Knighthood of the Bath" (London 1725)

Beeching, H.C., *Francis Atterbury* (1909)

Bevan, Bryan, *Marlborough the Man* A biography of John Churchill, first Duke of Marlborough (1975)

Bodley, John, *A Chapter of European and Imperial History* (1903)

Bingham, Madeleine, *Sheridan The Track of a Comet* (1972)

The Dairy of Mary Countess Cowper, Lady of the Bedchamber to the Princess of Wales (1864 edition)

Deutsch, Otto Erich, *Handel, A Documentary Biography* (1955)

Flower, Sir Newman, *George Frideric Handel, His Personality and his Times* (1959)

Gernsheim, Helmut and Alison, *Edward VII and Queen Alexandra*

Hervey, Lord George, *Memoirs* Vol. 1 & 2

Judd, Denis, *Palmerston* (1975)

Magnus-Allcroft, Sir Philip, *Edward VII* (1964)

Marie Louise H.H. Princess, *My Memory of Six Reigns* (1956)

Marshall, Dorothy, (General Ed. Antonia Fraser) *The Life and Times of Queen Victoria*

Marlow, Joyce, *Life and Times of George I* Introduction by A. Fraser (1973)

Prothero, G.W., *Life and Letters of Dean Stanley*. Vols I & II

Priestley, J.B. *The Prince of Pleasure and His Regency* 1811-1820. A Biography of the Prince Regent later George IV (1962)

Risk, James C., *The History of the Order of the Bath and its Insignia* (1972)

Smithers, Peter, *The Life of Joseph Addison* (1954)

Letters of Lady Augusta Stanley 1849-63. Edited by the Dean of Windsor and Hector

The Letters of Queen Victoria From Her Majesty's correspondence between the years 1837 and 1861. Vol. I. 1837-43

Woodham-Smith, Cecil, *Queen Victoria, Her Life and Times 1819-61*

Williams, Folkstone, *Memoirs and Correspondence of Francis Atterbury*. Vol. I (1909)

Ziegler, Philip, *William IV* (1971)

First Report of the Royal Commission appointed to inquire into the present lack of space for monuments in Westminster Abbey (1890)

The Spectator Vol. I. Printed from S. Buckley at the Dolphin in Little Britain, 1712, No. 26.

8

Windsor Monarchs and Westminster Abbey

During his brief reign, King Edward and Queen Alexandra made many state visits to France, Germany and elsewhere, working desperately for peace. As Edward lay dying on 6th May 1910, it was the generous and magnaminous gesture of Queen Alexandra, much commended by posterity, to bring Alice Keppel, a witty and brilliant woman and Edward's intimate friend during his last years, to her husband's bedside. He was already unconscious.

Edward VII's second son George now ascended the throne as George V, for his elder brother the Duke of Clarence had died many years earlier. It was a sagacious decision of the new King to choose Westminster Hall for his father's lying in state to satisfy the yearnings of the people to file past their beloved sovereign. It was an innovation, which has since become a tradition in the Royal Family. George was fortunate in his consort, the widely revered Queen Mary, formerly Princess May of Teck, who possessed superb dignity. I remember once many years ago standing on an island in the Mall, when the Queen passed in her car, bowing to right and left, and how deeply she impressed me.

George V was by temperament very religious, and the significance of his coronation obviously strongly affected him. It took place on Thursday, 22nd June 1911, a dull, but cloudy day. With his Queen beside him he drove in his great coach from Buckingham Palace to Westminster, dressed in his crimson robe of state. The King's train was borne by eight young pages. Troops from the Indian Empire, from East and West Africa, from Ceylon and Malaya, marched in the procession.

In the Abbey, George was crowned by the Archbishop of Canterbury, Randal Davidson, who afterwards paid homage for himself and on behalf of the Lords Spiritual. He was followed by Edward, Prince of Wales (the late Duke of Windsor), then a boy of seventeen, and the eager words promised much for the ensuing years. "I Edward Prince of Wales do become your liège man of life and limb, and of earthly worship, and faith and truth I will bear with you, to live and die against all manner of folks. So help me God."

For George V the solemn ritual was an act of dedication. In his biography of *George V, His Life and Reign*, Sir Harold Nicolson, allows the King to describe the scene in his own simple words. "There were over 50,000 troops lining the streets under the command of Lord Kitchener. The service in the Abbey was most beautiful, but it was a terrible ordeal. I nearly broke down when dear David came to do homage to me, as it reminded me so much when I did the same thing to beloved Papa, he did it so well. Darling May looked lovely, and it was indeed a comfort to me to have her by my side, as she has been ever to me during these last eighteen years." Queen Mary was then anointed and crowned.

James Pope-Hennessy, in his biography of Queen Mary, relates that Queen Alexandra was temporally haunted by a curious obsession that the 1911 coronation should have been by right that of her dead son, Prince Eddy (the Duke of Clarence) and not of King George: "Eddy should be King, not George," she kept repeating. Yet 'motherdear' as he called her, and George were absolutely devoted.

In her own way Queen Mary was as devout as her husband, and her reserved, yet sensitive nature was much stirred. James Pope-Hennessy quotes from a letter in the Royal Archives, which she wrote to her Aunt Augusta, Duchess of Mecklenburg-Strelitz: "To me who love tradition and the past, and who am English from top to toe, the service was a very real solemn thing and appealed to my feelings more than I can express – everything was most perfectly and reverently done – the foreigners seemed much impressed and were most nice and feeling ..." Who could have foretold in 1911 that the coronation of her grand-daughter, Queen Elizabeth II in 1952, would be televised, thus making its ritual familiar to millions of people?

Herbert Edward Ryle, who succeeded Armitage Robinson as Dean of Westminster, officiated at George V's coronation, and also at a number of royal marriages in the Abbey, including that of the Duke of York (later George VI) to the Lady Elizabeth-Bowes-Lyon in April 1923. It is greatly to Dean Ryle's credit that he had the imaginative sympathy to realize the significance of the burial of an unknown warrior in the Abbey after the first great war. Today people come from all parts of the Commonwealth to visit the grave of the Unknown Warrior in the nave. George V and his Queen attended the service on 11th November 1920, and other members of the Royal Family included the Prince of Wales, the Duke of York and Queen Alexandra.

It was in June 1920 that Dean Ryle appealed for £250,000 for the preservation of Westminster Abbey. Fifty-five years later Dean Edward Carpenter is today appealing for £8,000,000 for the much needed repair of the fabric. Prince Philip as President of the Abbey Trust, is actively promoting this project.

There is much talk of bombs today, and in the Abbey there is the necessity for constant vigilance and security. However, as far back as 11th June 1914 there was a bomb outrage by militant suffragists when the Coronation Chair and Stone of Destiny were slightly damaged.

On 27th February 1919, George V's cousin, Princess Patricia of Connaught (daughter of Arthur, Duke of Connaught) was married to Commander Ramsey (later Admiral Sir Alexander Ramsey), in Westminster Abbey. Another important wedding to take place in the Abbey three years later, was that of Princess Mary — the Princess Royal — to Viscount Lascelles (later the Earl of Harewood). The people delighted in the pageantry, and there was much popular enthusiasm. Her brother, the Duke of York, wrote the Prince of Wales, who was abroad, that the newspapers no longer described it as Mary's Wedding, but called it the "Abbey Wedding" or "The Royal Wedding" or the "National Wedding" or the "People's Wedding". The Princess Royal made a charming bride, performing her part to perfection as her mother thought. In the Abbey, the Queen Mother, Alexandra, now an old lady, was resplendent wearing violet velvet and the garter, and sparkling jewels.

When Albert, Duke of York, was about to marry the Lady Elizabeth Bowes-Lyon in Westminster Abbey, it was proposed by the B.B.C. that the services should be broadcast. Dean Ryle favoured this, but it was vetoed by the Chapter. Fifty years ago it was much too revolutionary and startling an idea. It took place on 26th April 1923, a fickle day characteristic of the English spring, clouds alternating with sunshine. Lady Elizabeth was very pretty, tactful and charming and likely to make Bertie, as the Duke of York was known in his family, a splendid wife. She was attended by six bridesmaids, while the bridegroom was supported by his elder brother the Prince of Wales and Prince Henry (the Duke of Gloucester). The Archbishop of Canterbury, Randall Davidson, solemnized the marriage, while the Archbishop of York made an eloquent address in which he especially referred to the Duke of York's work and interest in industrial relations. John Wheeler-Bennett in his biography of George VI, mentions the Archbishop's words: "You have made yourself at home in the mines and ship-yards and factories. You have brought the boys of the workshop and the public school together in free and frank companionship ..."

The Duke of York's younger brother the handsome Prince George, newly created Duke of Kent, married his beautiful bride Princess Marina of Greece on 29th November 1934, in Westminster Abbey. This was the first wedding to be broadcast to the nation. On the other hand Prince Henry, Duke of Gloucester, was married to his bride, Lady Alice Montagu-Douglas-Scott, a daughter of the Duke of Buccleuch, very quietly on 6th November 1935 in the Chapel of Buckingham Palace rather than Westminster Abbey, because the bride's father had recently died.

George V and Queen Mary often visited Westminster on official occasions, for instance on 17th July 1923 when they opened Westminster Hall on the completion of the restoration of the roof, which had continued for eight years. In was King George who re-inaugurated the Most Honourable Order of the Knights of the Bath in 1913, and his uncle, Arthur, Duke of Connaught, remained Great Master until his death in 1942.

After the decease of Dr Ryle in 1925, who was interred near the Unknown Warrior, he was succeeded by Dean Foxley Norris.

He was later to officiate at the coronation of George VI and Queen Elizabeth.

During November 1925 there died at Sandringham Queen Alexandra, and the funeral service, most beautiful and impressive, as Queen Mary considered, was held in Westminster Abbey on 27th November. Her body was then borne to Windsor where she was buried in the Memorial Chapel.

In 1928 Dr Cosmo Gordon Lang, a man of powerful personality, formerly Archbishop of York, was appointed Archbishop of Canterbury. He was to form an intimate friendship with George V during his later years, but he was later criticized for his uncharitable references to a few of the Duke of Windsor's friends, whose only fault had been loyalty to their master during the abdication crisis.

George V still ruled over a mighty Empire, and Westminster Abbey was increasingly regarded by the crowds who visited the Collegiate Church of St Peter as its 'heart-shrine', as Dean Ryle wrote in a supplement of *The Times* in 1920. There they came from all parts of the Empire, from Australia, Canada, New Zealand and South Africa. Their enthusiasm, their emotion, and their feeling for the historic associations of the place inspired those, who had the privilege of conducting them. The Americans, too, love the Abbey with a deep, true, abiding affection. I have seen tears pour down their cheeks as they are overwhelmed by its beauty.

George V was a sagacious, constitutional King, immensely hard-working and conscientious, but lacking the intuition and imaginative sympathy to understand the changed conditions in England after the First World War. Nor did he possess his father's expert knowledge of Europe, or aspire to excel as an arbiter of peace as Edward VII certainly did. He was made of a simpler mould, and his loyalty was to the country he served so devotedly both in peace and war. His character had been formed in early manhood during his naval career. King George possessed a superb voice for radio and those who heard him are not likely to forget it.

During the winter of 1928, George V was extremely ill, and after his recovery, together with Queen Mary, he attended a service of thanksgiving in Westminster Abbey on Sunday, 7th

July 1929. John W. Wheeler-Bennett related in his biography of George VI, that this service and broadcast all over the world. "Fancy a thanksgiving service with an open wound in your back", commented the King to his physician Lord Dawson of Penn, after his return to the Palace.

In January 1936 George V's life was fast ebbing towards its close and he was succeeded by his eldest son Edward, Prince of Wales, as Edward VIII, a man who had travelled widely in all parts of the world. For George V there was the lying in state in Westminster Hall, when the great silent crowds filed past. Officers of the Brigade of Guards watched over the coffin. The new King endeared himself to the people by an imaginative gesture. For a while he and his three brothers in the uniform of their respective services, kept the last vigil over their father's catafalque. How well I recollect as a young man, standing in St James's Street on that winter day as the four brothers, Edward VIII, the Dukes of York, Gloucester and Kent, all with set faces, walked in the funeral procession as George V was borne to his grave in St George's Chapel, Windsor.

The coronation of Edward VIII had been arranged for 12th May 1937, but before the end of 1936 the King had signed the instrument of abdication, determined to marry Mrs Wallis Simpson, the woman whom he loved. He went into exile, and was created Duke of Windsor by the Duke of York at his accession council, who now succeeded him as George VI.

George VI resembled his father in character, rather than his grandfather, though naturally he was far more modern in outlook. In some ways the new King curiously resembled his great-grandfather, the Prince Consort, particularly in his conscientiousness, his tendency to overwork and to worry over details, his essential modesty and the feelings of inadequacy which afflicted him at times. He was to prove a successful king, which shows at least the value of a naval training for a prince destined to ascend the throne, however reluctant he may be.

In their discussions with Dr Lang, the King and Queen supported his view that their coronation should be broadcast, though some opposed the broadcasting of the service within the Abbey. The King was eager that the people throughout the Commonwealth should share in the spiritual experience of the coronation. The Earl Marshal, the late Duke of Norfolk, did not favour the televising of the ceremony, and others no doubt opposed it. Various important changes were introduced into the order of service. The Litany no longer formed part of the service, but was chanted by the Westminster Canons as they walked in procession down from the altar before the coronation. There was no sermon at George VI's coronation. It was decided to restore the former order of the anointing, where the Sovereign was anointed on the hands upwards to the head. As John W. Wheeler-Bennett mentions in his biography of George VI, there was a further change affecting the oath. When George V was crowned, this part of the ceremony had occurred after the beginning of the Communion Service. It was now restored to its ancient place immediately after the recognition. For the recognition the words "of this realm" were omitted, and the King was presented to his people as "King George your undoubted King" reflecting the altered status of the King's self-governing dominions as provided by the Statute of Westminster. George VI and his Queen were crowned on 12th May 1937.

Tradition meant much to the Queen Mother, Mary, and an ancient tradition reputed to date from the reigns of Plantagenet sovereigns is that British Queens do not attend the coronation of their husband's successor. Queen Adelaide had not attended her niece Victoria's coronation, while Queen Alexandra had remained at Sandringham when her son was crowned. Queen Mary, however, was well aware that the monarchy had survived a terrible crisis. She thought that her presence might consolidate the throne, and she asked her son's permission to attend in Westminster Abbey. She sat next to her sister-in-law, Queen Maud in the royal box. She described her grandchildren Princess Elizabeth (Lilibet) then aged eleven, and Princess Margaret a girl of seven, looking "too sweet in their lace dresses and robes, especially when they put on their coronets".

The day 12th May was dull and overcast. The King and Queen left for the Abbey just after half past ten, in the State Coach built for George III in 1762. It was drawn by eight Windsor greys. As they entered the west door of the Abbey, the Westminster Choir sang the anthem, "I was glad when they said unto me". For such a shy retiring man as George VI, for he never sought the limelight, the strain must have been immense. The magnificent voice of Archbishop Lang resounded: "Sire, I here present unto you King George, your undoubted King ..." and the congregation answered with one voice: "God save the King."

George VI's own account written as a memorial is not without humour and slight irony. There were a number of mishaps. Foxley Norris, the Dean of Westminster, was insisting that the King should put on the white Colobium Sindonis, a surplice, inside out when George's groom of the Robes came to the rescue. When he was kneeling at the Altar to take the coronation oath, the King's two supporters, the Bishops of Bath and Wells, and Durham, were unable to find the words. "Horror of horrors," wrote the King, when "the Archbishop held his book down for me to read, his thumbs covered the words of the Oath." Worse was to follow. George was obliged to fix the belt of his sword himself because the Lord Great Chamberlain fumbled with it so much that his hands shook. The King, who was inclined to worry and fret about detail, was naturally anxious that the crown should be set on his head with the right side to the front. To help the Archbishop, a little piece of red cotton had been put under one of the principal jewels on the crown. The crowning and the anointing are the supreme moments of the coronation, but Archbishop Lang was momentarily nonplussed when putting St Edward's Crown, which weighs seven pounds, on the King's head, not to be able to find the thread of red cotton on the crown. Some officious person had removed it before the ceremony. "I never did know whether it was right or not," wrote the King. Then one of the bishops trod on George's robes after the King arose from the coronation chair. "I had to tell him to get off it pretty sharply as I nearly fell down," related the King.

Perhaps His Majesty, speaking in an undertone, used naval language. No mishaps marred the crowning of George's radiant Queen Consort Elizabeth. When Archbishop Lang set the crown upon her head, he said: "Receive the Crown of Glory, Honour and Joy."

One Prime Minister buried in Westminster Abbey, beneath a pew in the nave, during the reign of George VI, was Neville Chamberlain, a controversial character, but a man who worked diligently for peace. The King had been attached to Neville

Chamberlain, and his younger brother Henry, Duke of Gloucester attended the funeral on 14th November 1940, as George VI's personal representative. Rudyard Kipling, a great poet and story-teller when the British Empire was at its zenith, died in 1936. He was interred in Poets' Corner, and Stanley Baldwin, who was related to him acted as a pall-bearer at his funeral. Near Kipling lie the ashes of Thomas Hardy, author of *Far From The Madding Crowd*, and other famous novels. His heart is buried, however, in Slinsford Churchyard in his native Dorset. Hardy really belongs to an earlier era, for he died in 1928. Clement Attlee, Prime Minister after the 1939-45 war and his Foreign Secretary, Ernest Bevin, are both interred in the Abbey.

In the course of World War II (1942) there died Queen Victoria's last surviving son, Arthur, Duke of Connaught. He was succeeded in the office of Great Master of the Most Honourable Order of the Knights of the Bath, by Henry, Duke of Gloucester, who was to hold this post for thirty-two years until his decease in the summer of 1974. It was George VI, who went to the Abbey in state on 24th May 1951, to install the Duke of Gloucester as Great Master at a special service in King Henry VII's Chapel. This installation, certainly one of the most beautiful ceremonies to take place in the Abbey, was the first to be held during George VI's reign. No service attended by a sovereign had taken place since 1928, when George V was present. On the occasion when George VI installed his brother, he presented his own sword to Dr Alan Don, then Dean of Westminster, who first placed it on the altar and shortly afterwards returned it to the King. This is the same sword, much admired by visitors, which was, after George VI's death in 1952, returned to the Abbey by Queen Elizabeth II and the Queen Mother and is now in the Henry VII Chapel.

The Dean of Westminster during the Second World War was Dr de Labilliere and his spirit of resolute patriotism inspired the Abbey through these years of crisis. He ordered the Union Jack to be flown on the Abbey flagpole for six years until the war ended. Although his Deanery was mainly destroyed in 1941, according to *A House of Kings*, he stayed on there, and did not often leave London during those years.

Visitors from overseas often enquire whether the Abbey was

bombed and whether much damage was sustained. The magnificent stained glass above Chaucer's monument, was destroyed, while during a raid in September 1940, the great west window was damaged. The roof of the lantern also caught fire on a later occasion, and fell on to the pavement below. It was miraculous that no other serious damage occurred at the time, and nobody was injured. However, the lantern which replaced it, is very beautiful, especially from within the building. There was severe damage to houses in the beautiful Little Cloisters, particularly to No. 6, and despite the massive effort of the fire brigade, it could not be saved. Surely the Abbey's guardian angels watched over the ancient building, so that it has been preserved to delight future generations.

Starved of pageantry during the war years, the people spontaneously warmed to the light and colour of Princess Elizabeth's marriage to Lieutenant Philip Mountbatten, created Duke of Edinburgh, which took place in Westminster Abbey on 20th November 1947. Dr Alan Don had succeeded Dr de Labilliere as Dean of Westminster, and he assisted Geoffrey Fisher, Archbishop of Canterbury, at the wedding.

Princess Elizabeth with her father, drove to the Abbey in the Irish State Coach. In the Abbey she was attended by eight bridesmaids, including Princess Margaret and Princess Alexandra of Kent. Just before the King entered with the Princess, a fanfare of silver trumpets sounded in King Henry V's Chantry, above St Edward's Shrine. Among those already in the Abbey were foreign kings and queens and leaders of the nation and Empire, including Mackenzie King and General Smuts. As Winston Churchill, then Leader of the Opposition, walked alone to his stall in the choir, everybody in the nave rose to honour him.

The Special Correspondent of *The Times* in his description of the ceremonial on 21st November, quaintly wrote, for he had a strong sense of history, "Of the royal ladies of the past, only Aveline of Lancaster (married to a younger son of Henry III in the Abbey) lies so close to the sanctuary that one might imagine her pathetic ghost looking out from her canopied tomb to wish her remote successor longer life and better fortune than fate measured out to her."

Behind the bride, holding her train, came her two pages,

Prince William of Gloucester and Prince Michael of Kent, both in white shirts and scarlet kilts. When the pages later got entangled with the train, the King, with a characteristic gesture, stooped to help them.

Dr Geoffrey Fisher, Archbishop of Canterbury, conducted the most important part of the service. When he asked, "Who giveth this woman?" George VI took the Princess's right hand in his own, and then yielded it to the Duke of Edinburgh. Dr Cyril Garbett, Archbishop of York, gave an address. After the register had been signed, in St Edward's Chapel, trumpets once again sounded from King Henry V's Chantry. David Duff in his *Elizabeth of Glamis* relates an amusing incident as the King and Queen came out of the Abbey. King Feisal could not resist inspecting the bridal coach and the horses, so a policeman not recognizing His Majesty and thinking him merely a prying boy took him under his care. He was rescued by an equerry.

George VI was only to live scarcely more than three more years. He was an excellent constitutional King, in the image of his father, and he had been sustained through favourable times and adversity by his devoted wife. They both owed much to one another. His health, like the Prince Consort's, had never been robust, and after a very serious operation his condition gave acute anxiety. He died suddenly at Sandringham on 6th February 1952, where he had been born on 14th December 1895, the anniversary of the Prince Consort's death, after whom he had been named Albert.

Once again a sovereign lay in state in Westminster Hall, while the great and the humble filed solemnly past, glancing perhaps for a moment at the beautiful hammer-beam roof above.

So, our Queen Elizabeth II mounted the throne to reign over England, ascending it at twenty-five, the same age as her illustrious namesake, Elizabeth I.

BIBLIOGRAPHY

Duff, David, *Elizabeth of Glamis* (1973)
Nicholson, Harold, *King George V His Life and Reign* (1952)
Pope-Hennessy, James, *Queen Mary* (1959)
Wheeler-Bennett, Sir John W., *King George VI* (1958)

10

Westminster Abbey Today

One of the most traditional and interesting services held sometimes in the Abbey, is the Royal Maundy service. Our Queen when Princess Elizabeth and aged only nine, first attended it with her mother the Duchess of York in 1935. Since 1952, when she became Queen, she has often distributed the Maundy both in Westminster Abbey and other churches throughout the country. More of Royal Maundy anon.

Unlike the coronation of her father, which had merely been broadcast on sound radio, Queen Elizabeth II's coronation on 2nd June, 1953, was on television, thus reaching a much wider audience both at home and throughout the Commonwealth.

The most sacred part of the ritual is the anointing, and it was seemly that it should be veiled from the sight of millions of viewers. Such moments are too sacred for intrusion. The anthem "Zadok the Priest" was sung before the anointing. Four Knights of the Garter in their mantles of blue velvet, held the canopy over the head of their Queen, as Archbishop Fisher, together with Dean Alan Don came towards her from the altar, the Dean as was customary, carrying the ampulla in the form of an eagle, and the spoon. The Archbishop anointed Elizabeth II upon her hands, her breast and upon her head with holy oil, speaking the words of consecration aloud.

For the millions of viewers on television the most dramatic moment is when the Archbishop of Canterbury lifts St Edward's Crown and reverently sets it on her head, and "it descended gently in all the flashing splendour of sovereignty on the youthful brow, bowed to receive it", as the correspondent of *The Times* wrote. No mishaps marred the Queen's coronation, but it was a nervous few moments for the Archbishop.

One of the highlights is when the Westminster scholars shout *Vivat Regina, Vivat Regina Elizabeth, Vivat, Vivat, Vivat*. Another grand moment was when Philip, Duke of Edinburgh, knelt before his Queen, and his wife, to perform his act of homage, to swear among other things to become her liège man of life and limb and of earthly worship.

The sword of state, one of the emblems of chivalry, was borne on this day by the late Marquess of Salisbury, and it is the custom for it to be carried before the Queen at various stages of the ceremony. Then Lord Salisbury exchanged the sword of state for a sword in a jewelled scabbard, which he gave to the Archbishop. Meanwhile the Lord Chamberlain, Lord Scarborough, bore the sword of state into St Edward's Chapel behind the high altar. Archbishop Fisher, together with the Archbishop of York and other church dignitaries, gave the jewelled sword to the Queen, admonishing her to do justice, stop the growth of iniquity and to defend widows and orphans, among other things. Queen Elizabeth II then rose from her chair, and walked to the altar where she surrendered the sword, signifying that she now conceded temporal power into God's keeping. The jewelled sword, unlike the state sword, is the Sovereign's personal property, and this was redeemed at the altar by Lord Salisbury. To redeem it he produced an embroidered bag containing a hundred shillings freshly minted. It is the custom for these shillings to be distributed among the clergy and officers of Westminster Abbey after the coronation service.

One person missing from her grand-daughter's coronation was the Queen Dowager, Mary, who would have delighted in the ritual. Alas! she had died earlier in 1952. Prince Charles, Duke of Cornwall, not yet created Prince of Wales, an excited little boy, sat between his grandmother Elizabeth, the Queen Mother and his aunt, Princess Margaret in the front row of the Royal Gallery, eagerly asking them questions. One day, the Prince of Wales – God willing – closely associated as he already is with the Abbey as Great Master of the Knights of the Bath, will be crowned King.

When the Queen and her supporters, the Bishops of Durham, and Bath and Wells, proceeded through the nave to the west door of Westminster Abbey, after the end of the service, she was wearing, as is customary the Imperial State Crown,* holding the orb and sceptre. The choral music was conducted by Dr McKie (later Sir William) a fine musician, and Bax's "Coronation March" and part of Elgar's "Pomp and Circumstance" Marches, greeted the Queen as she left the Abbey. The loyal acclamations of her subjects were none the less fervent, despite the dismal rain pouring from leaden skies.

Our Queen has started an interesting innovation in arranging that the Royal Maundy services should be held not only in Westminster Abbey, but at churches throughout the country. For instance in 1957, it was held in St Albans, indeed for the first time outside London for two hundred years, at Rochester in 1961, and again at Westminster Abbey in 1962. The Queen does not always distribute the Maundy, for instance in 1964 when Eric Abbot was Dean of Westminster, the Queen asked her aunt the late Princess Royal to do so on her behalf. How appropriate it was that this traditional service should be held at Tewkesbury in Gloucestershire, in 1971, the 500th anniversary of the Battle of Tewkesbury during the Wars of the Roses. It has also taken place in Durham. A booklet on *The Pictorial History of the Royal Maundy*, by Peter H. Wright, secretary of the Royal Almonry, relates its historical importance. King John, not noted for his piety, took part in the Maundy ceremony in 1213, at Rochester when he gave thirteen pence to each of thirteen men. We have already mentioned Henry V, a deeply religious man taking part in a Royal Maundy service in 1412 at Langley in Hertfordshire, when he distributed 4d. a piece to 3,000 poor people. It was his father Henry IV who started the custom relating the number of recipients to the sovereign's age. Queen Elizabeth II will be aged fifty in 1976, so that there should be fifty recipients.

There are few mentions of the distribution of the Royal Maundy in the days of the Stuarts, but an entry at Somerset House named "Chapels Royal Register – Births, Deaths, Marriages," say: "On Maundy Thursday, 16th April 1685, our gracious King James ye 2nd, was'd, wip'd, and kiss'd the feet of

---

* Among its jewels is the balas ruby known as the Black Prince's ruby traditionally, given to him by Pedro the Cruel, King of Castile, after the Prince's victory at Najera in 1367.

52 poor men with wonderful humility ..." Charles II, too, a very popular King took part in the ancient ritual. The ceremony was formerly held in the Chapel Royal in Whitehall, but from 1891 onwards for sixty years, it took place in Westminster Abbey, although occasionally held elsewhere. For many years, however, no reigning King took part in the Royal Maundy until George V was present in the Abbey in 1932 to donate the traditional red and white purses in the second distribution. Four years later Edward VII distributed the purses while he was on the throne. George VI also took a marked interest in the Royal Maundy and distributed the gifts on seven occasions. Like his father, he did not care to delegate what he considered was his own duty to another member of the Royal Family. If he was absent, an official called the Lord High Almoner represented him at the Maundy service. Among the Lord High Almoners was a former outstanding Dean of Westminster, Armitage Robinson, who after he left the Abbey in 1911, to become Dean of Wells, returned there in his official capacity on several occasions to perform these duties.

The Abbey is increasingly important today for its international flavour, and citizens visit it from throughout the Commonwealth, inspired by its various services. Nobody who attended the eve of Commonwealth service held on 14th June 1974, when the Prince of Wales was present, is likely to forget the experience, nor the eager interest he showed in the playing of the sitar by Ravi Shankar, and other music. Representatives from every part of the world were present, including the United Kingdom, Australia, India, Sri Lanka, New Zealand, Ghana, Uganda, Nigeria, Canada, Malaysia, Malta, Barbados, Bahamas, Jamaica, Swaziland, Trinidad and Tobago, Tonga and Cyprus. The music before the service by the Enfield citadel Band of the Salvation Army included works by Handel, Purcell and Elgar's "Nimrod" from the *Enigma Variations*.

Another important service to be held in the summer of 1974, was the Festal Evensong for the installation of Dr Edward Carpenter as Dean of the Collegiate Church of St Peter. At this service the officers of the Most Honourable Order of the Bath proceeded in stately fashion from the Chapel of St George along the nave to their seats in the lantern. The Lord Mayor, and the Aldermen and Councillors of the City of Westminster, attended on this occasion, so did the Lord Chancellor Lord Elwin-Jones, a dignified figure whose train was gallantly borne by a tiny attendant. The music before the service included Handel's exquisite *Water Music*, and there were fanfares played by trumpeters from the Royal Military School of Music, Kneller Hall.

Memorial services take place fairly often in the Abbey today, though funerals are very rare. The most important on 23rd July 1974 commemorated the Duke of Gloucester, Great Master of the Knights of the Bath, and members of the Most Honourable Order, naturally took a prominent part in the procession. His widow, Alice, Duchess of Gloucester, was present together with her son Prince Richard, the new Duke and his Danish-born wife, also Princess Alexandra of Kent and her husband Angus Ogilvie. My chief memories are the beauty of the music, particularly of the Purcell "When I am Laid in the Earth", and Bach's "Jesu, Joy of Man's Desiring". The responses were sung to the music of the Abbey's organist and Master of the Choristers, Douglas Guest. Before the service, Dr Ramsey, the Archbishop of Canterbury, soon to retire, looked a strangely lonely, though human person, seated by himself in the nave. It was the Archbishop who pronounced the blessing. After the service in the Abbey, bells were rung, half-muffled. A typical memorial service was that of the distinguished soldier, Field Marshal Robertson. In September a service of thanksgiving took place for the distinguished Prime Minister of New Zealand, Norman Kirke.

I attended the Festal Evensong to welcome the new Archbishop of Canterbury, Dr Frederick Coggan, held in the Abbey on 25th January, which commemorates the conversion of St Paul, and Dr Coggan referred to that apostle in his address. The Archbishop of Canterbury has no right of choir in the Abbey, only during the ceremony of the coronation. A special Evensong takes place for senior citizens of the City of Westminster, and this service is usually attended by the Lord Mayor of Westminster. An important annual thanksgiving service to honour the men who won the Battle of Britain, is held annually in September and in 1975 Baroness Spencer-Churchill, widow of the great Sir Winston Churchill, was present together with her daughter Sarah Lady Audley. He is interred in the quiet graveyard of Bladon, in Oxfordshire, but a marble stone in the nave commemorates him.

When the Queen comes to the Abbey as an official visitor, she sits in her own stall at the back of the choir (usually kept for the Dean), where there is a royal coat of arms. For instance, she sat there on 11th November 1975 on the occasion of the inauguration of the 1975-1980 General Synod of the Church of England. At royal weddings the Queen sits in one of the chairs presented by the Canadian Government, raised a little higher than the one occupied by Prince Philip.

There was seldom a dull moment when I served as a temporary marshal in the Abbey during the spring and summer of 1974. On the night of 4th September there was a daring attempt by a young Scottish Nationalist, David Carmichael-Stewart, living in Wolverhampton, to steal the Stone of Scone, which is affixed to the Coronation Chair. The man managed to conceal himself in the St Edward's Chapel on the night of Wednesday 4th September, when the Abbey is normally open to visitors until 8 p.m. He succeeded in wrenching the heavy sandstone block out of the Coronation Chair and was loading it on to a trolley when the alarm bell rang. Numerous police converged on the Abbey, and Carmichael-Stewart was arrested. At Bow Street he was later conditionally discharged for a year and ordered to pay £150 and £75 costs. The Coronation Chair would cost £150 to repair since damage had been done to its panelling and batons.

Earlier in June great palls of smoke lay over Westminster Hall after a bomb had been planted by the I.R.A. Fortunately, however, the damage was slight to the building, though several people were injured.

In the Abbey itself there were fairly frequent bomb scares throughout that exciting summer, and we were given careful instructions to report suspicious packages or carrier bags to the Dean's Verger, Mr Greaves. On occasions like the Duke of Gloucester's memorial service, Abbey security bring in their labradors, highly trained to sniff in case of possible explosives. Most of our visitors are very well behaved, but I was aghast on one occasion during that uneasy summer to see a man puffing at a cigar as he crossed the bridge into the St Edward's Chapel. With my stern eye upon him he did not require a second warning. The prominent notices displayed "No Ices in the Abbey" have not altogether deterred people from infringing this regulation.

One personality, who will be sadly missed in the Abbey when he retires at the end of 1975 to live in Islip, Oxfordshire is Mr Algy Greaves, Dean's Verger for many years, a witty and kindly man.

The Dean and Chapter have a session every fortnight in the Jerusalem Chamber of Westminster Abbey, except for the months of August and September. The Receiver-General, Mr W.R.J. Pullen is present on these occasions and red cassocks and gowns are generally worn. The Dean of Westminster is the Chairman of the Dean and Chapter, the governing body of the Abbey. He is the sole authority for special services. If a proposal was made to change the form of service, it is a matter for the present Dean, Dr Edward Carpenter. The Dean of Westminster is the sole authority for deciding on burials, but these are very rare today. However, in practice he would consult the Chapter.

Today marriages sometimes take place in the King Henry VII Chapel — a lovely setting for a wedding — and the Dean again decides on these. It may well be that the daughter or son of the Most Honourable of the Knights of the Bath is married in this Chapel, or the daughter of an official employed by the Abbey, who has devoted many years of service to the Church of St Peter. Royal marriages, are of course a matter for the Queen, and the wedding of her daughter Princess Anne to Mark Philips in the Abbey on 4th November 1973 is too recent to need any comment, having been televised all over the world. Dr Eric Abbott, when Dean of Westminster, assisted the Archbishop of Canterbury, Dr Fisher at the marriage of the Queen's sister, Princess Margaret with Anthony Armstrong-Jones on 6th May 1960, later created Lord Snowdon. He also officiated at the wedding of Princess Alexandra to the Hon. Angus Ogilvie on 24th April 1963.

It is, perhaps, little known that coronation day is the only occasion when Westminster Abbey is removed from the jurisdiction of the Dean and Chapter. An Order in Council is necessary. Keys are then surrendered to the Earl Marshal, a hereditary position held by the Dukes of Norfolk. The Abbey authorities are required to give access to the Department of the Environment.

The Canons in residence are always appointed by the Queen on the advice of the Prime Minister. It is important to emphasize the Abbey's spiritual significance in the heart of the nation, primarily as a place of worship. Every hour throughout the day the chaplains call for silence and suitable prayers are said lasting for two minutes.

Wreath-laying ceremonies at the tomb of the Unknown Soldier often take place. Various societies, too, such as the Dickens Fellowship, the Byron Society, the Faucett Society and the Samuel Johnson Society, commemorate the anniversaries of the great writers or poets, whom they wish to honour, by laying wreaths on their tablets or graves. On Battle of Britain Day, 15th September, the R.A.F. lay a wreath on the grave of Lord Dowding.

There is so much beauty and harmony, enhanced by the elegance of the sixteen Waterford glass chandeliers presented to the Abbey by members of the Guinness family in 1965, to commemorate the 900th anniversary of the consecration of the Church of Edward the Confessor. The stone work of the Rose Window in the south transept was the work of Sir Gilbert Scott in 1849, an architect of distinction whose work conferred great benefit on the Abbey.

Hoary with age, history is being made in the Abbey all the time, and here lies its everlasting fascination. After his installation as Great Master of the Most Honourable Order of the Bath, at the end of May 1975, the Prince of Wales told a leading participant how much he had enjoyed the ceremonial. Since he possesses imaginative sympathy and a keen sense of history, the Prince's associations with the Abbey will become even more intimate in the ensuing years.

BIBLIOGRAPHY

The Times, 3rd June 1953

Wright, Peter H., *Pictorial History of the Royal Maundy*

Index